SEXUALITY,
DISABILITY,
AND AGING

D1616142

SEXUALITY, DISABILITY, AND AGING

Queer Temporalities of the Phallus

JANE GALLOP

Duke University Press   Durham and London   2019

Library of Congress Cataloging-in-Publication Data
Names: Gallop, Jane, [date] author.
Title: Sexuality, disability, and aging :
queer temporalities of the phallus / Jane Gallop.
Description: Durham : Duke University Press, 2019. |
Includes bibliographical references and index.
Identifiers: LCCN 2018020448 (print)
LCCN 2018034091 (ebook)
ISBN 9781478002697 (ebook)
ISBN 9781478001263 (hardcover : alk. paper)
ISBN 9781478001614 (pbk. : alk. paper)
Subjects: LCSH: People with disabilities—Sexual behavior.
| Sociology of disability. | Disability studies. | Queer theory.
| Older people—Sexual behavior. | Sex (Psychology)
Classification: LCC HQ30.5 (ebook) |
LCC HQ30.5 .G35 2019 (print) |
DDC 362.4—dc23
LC record available at https://lccn.loc.gov/2018020448

COVER ART: Aaron Paul Rogers, 2018. Courtesy of the artist.

This book is dedicated to my father

MELVIN GALLOP (1923–2017)

my role model in aging

as I watched him become less anxious and more happy

in his advanced age

CONTENTS

ACKNOWLEDGMENTS

Over the seven years that I worked on this book, I benefited greatly from the help of three research assistants, doctoral students here at the University of Wisconsin–Milwaukee. They helped me find relevant texts, often remote from my or their field of study, and gave me constructive feedback on my early drafts. This book is much better because of their help. I want here to acknowledge my enormous good fortune for having such smart and insightful assistance, and to thank Bob Bruss, Shawna Lipton, and Ali Sperling for their work, their criticism, and their encouragement.

Three friends offered me invaluable feedback at different stages of this book; these three are not only dear friends but ideal colleagues. I am grateful to Greg Jay, Caroline Levine, and Ted Martin for their generous help.

I cannot possibly express appropriate thanks to Dick Blau, life partner of four decades, for his support of this book. Without his willingness to risk exposure in these pages, this book simply could not be what it is. Dick is many wonderful things, but here I'd like to thank him for being such a good sport.

THEORETICAL
UNDERPINNINGS

Crip Theory

Over the last two decades there has been a flourishing of writing at the intersection of queer theory and disability studies. I will here be calling this intersectional discourse "crip theory," after Robert McRuer's 2006 book, *Crip Theory: Cultural Signs of Queerness and Disability*.[1] The first time I saw McRuer's title, I immediately loved the attitudinal kinship of "crip" with "queer" and felt that was the direction I wanted my theorizing to head.

The intersection with disability studies has become one of the liveliest sites in twenty-first-century queer theory. Most strikingly, within queer theory, disability studies is not a special-interest application, but an advance in theorizing queer. For example, Eli Clare writes:

> My first experience of queerness centered not on sexuality or gender, but on disability. Early on, I understood my body to be irrevocably different from those of my . . . playmates . . . a body that moved slow, wrists cocked at odd angles, muscles knotted with tremors. . . . I heard: "wrong, broken . . . unacceptably queer" . . . as my classmates called out *cripple, re-*

tard. . . . This was my first experience of queerness. Only later came gender and sexuality. Again I found my body to be irrevocably different. At nine, ten, eleven, my deepest sense of self was as neither boy nor girl.[2]

This quotation from Clare exemplifies what I find most exciting about the intersection of queer and disability theory. Disability here *is* queer, queerer than queer, a more powerful way to resist normativity, a more radical affirmation of bodily difference.

The present book began with my reading a lot of crip theory. This book is, first and foremost, rooted in the way crip theory resonates with my own experience as someone who, since the beginning of the twenty-first century, has slowly been losing the ability to walk or even stand—with my experience as a part-time wheelchair user. As a scholar in queer theory, I found disability an attractive identity and a compelling theoretical move.

I have been particularly drawn to a tendency in disability studies that valorizes what Rosemarie Garland-Thomson has memorably called "extraordinary bodies," a tendency to "claim physical difference as exceptional rather than inferior."[3] For an explicitly sexual example of this viewpoint in which disabled comes off as superior to the norm, I would cite the disabled woman who, when surveyed for a study of sex and disability, responded: "If you are a sexually active disabled person . . . it is remarkable how dull and unimaginative non-disabled people's sex lives can appear."[4]

When disability becomes overtly queer, we find provocations such as Riva Lehrer's in the 2012 volume *Sex and Disability*: "I will be one of the crip girls whose bodies scare the panel of judges. They are afraid that our unbalanced shapes hint of unsanctioned desires. On both sides of the bed."[5] For those of us who glory in the threateningly antinormative, "crip" can look like a wildly sexy identity.

What I am here calling crip theory includes not just twenty-first-century work in explicit interaction with queer theory but also writing from the "disability sex rights movement" of the 1990s.[6] Although this work by social scientists is less well known to those of us in the humanities, it paves the way for queer writing on disability and shares the pro-sex antinormativity that for me is the hallmark of crip theory.

Anthropologist Emily Wentzell explains this movement thus: "In keeping with the disability movement's celebration of 'crip culture' . . . the disability sex movement sought to champion non-normative forms of sexual expression developed by . . . individuals with specific impairments."[7] For example, in a review published in 1996 Barbara Waxman and Carol Gill refer to "the different sexual styles . . . inspired by disabilities" and "the rich and creative array of . . . sexual behaviors and expressive styles that persons with disabilities have developed."[8] Waxman and Gill's language here bespeaks both the appreciation for plural sexualities ("rich . . . array") and the emphasis on the agency and creativity of disabled people that characterize crip theory.

A major figure in the 1990s disability sex movement, sociologist Tom Shakespeare, considers what the movement is doing as analogous to queer. In an article in *Sexuality and Disability*, Shakespeare writes: "In exploring disabled sexuality, we are faced by similar questions to the lesbian and gay . . . scholars who have explored gay and queer sexual politics. Are we trying to win access for disabled people to the mainstream of sexuality, or are we trying to challenge the ways in which sex and sexuality are conceived . . . and limited in modern societies?"[9] While conceding that many disabled men and women opt for the first choice (trying for access to the mainstream), Shakespeare comes down definitively on the side of the second option. This choice aligns him with "queer sexual politics"; it makes him and his colleagues part of crip theory.

In the same article, Shakespeare articulates the theoretical ambitions of what I am here calling crip theory: "We can . . . challenge a whole lot of ideas that predominate in the sexual realm, and enable others—not just disabled people—to reassess what is important and what is possible." Rather than trying to join the mainstream, the disability sex movement could "enable others—not just disabled people"—to move beyond limited conceptions of sexuality. Shakespeare suggests one form that challenge could take: "Disabled people can challenge the obsession with fitness and youth."[10] Who is not constrained and oppressed by this obsession?

My notion of crip theory not only includes those thinking about disability within the framework of queer theory; it not only includes social scientists in the disability sex rights movement. As used here, it also includes scholars theorizing from a similar position, even though not explicitly connected either to queer theory or to disability studies. For example, I was surprised and pleased to find what I could call crip theory in an article from 2013 in the journal *Cancer Nursing* authored by researchers from the School of Medicine at the University of Western Sydney.

In this article, "Renegotiating Sex and Intimacy after Cancer," Jane M. Ussher, Janette Perz, Emilee Gilbert, W. K. Tim Wong, and Kim Hobbs write: "Rather than the cancer-affected body being positioned as site of illness, failure or abjection, it can be conceptualized as a 'key site of transgression,' serving to break the boundaries that define sex within a narrow, heteronormative framework."[11] Rather than the cancer-affected body being considered pitiful or inferior, it can provide us with a theoretical resource, a conceptual basis from which to challenge the normative sexual framework. Although Ussher and her colleagues have no citations from queer theory or disability studies, their qualitative study of the renegotiation of sex by individuals with cancer finds its way to a very queer, very crip conclusion.

While I will go on to elucidate a number of other theoretical discussions underpinning the present book, I begin here with crip theory, not only because that is where this project began but also because it remains the fundamental theoretical perspective throughout the book. Whatever theoretical complications and explorations follow, I want to begin by grounding us in an affirmation of "the rich and creative array of . . . sexual behaviors and expressive styles" arising from nonnormative bodies and especially in the way such bodies can "challenge a whole lot of ideas that predominate in the sexual realm."[12]

Aging and Queer Temporality

The crip theory framework I originally envisioned for this book began to change in January 2013, even before I started writing. In the hotel lobby at the convention of the Modern Language Association (MLA), I found myself by chance standing next to Devoney Looser and a couple other people who were discussing a session for the next year's convention, a session that would be called "Age and/as Disability." Eavesdropping unabashedly, I came to realize something that had not occurred to me before. For more than a decade, I had been dealing with a progressive disability that began at the age of forty-nine; yet, up until that moment, I had thought of my situation *only* as disability, not as aging. Wanting to do writing based in this experience, I had been drawn to crip theory; it had never occurred to me to turn to aging studies.

There is, I have since learned, a wide swath where the categories of disability and aging bleed into each other. As Michael Bérubé, a leading figure in disability studies, puts it: "The fact that many of us will become disabled if we live long enough is perhaps the fundamental aspect of human embodiment."[13] Statements like this are found everywhere in disability studies, suggesting a widespread recognition that disability as a category is entangled with aging. The gesture toward this overlap appears in aging studies as well. For example, Margaret Morganroth Gullette, an important theorist of aging, remarks: "Without stereotyping old age or ignoring disabilities at younger ages, one can conclude that people are likely to have special needs as they age into middle and later life."[14] Yet, despite the frequency of this gesture, there is little critical or theoretical work that draws from both disability and aging studies.

Thanks to that chance hotel lobby encounter early in 2013, this book benefits from both of these theoretical frameworks. My focus here is in fact what Gullette terms "special needs as [people] age into middle and later life": the swath of experience that can be understood either as disability or as aging, the experience of what I will call late-onset disability, disability beginning in the middle years or beyond.

Back in 2013, as I eavesdropped at the MLA convention, I found myself wondering why I had never considered aging for this project. Why, as a queer theorist, had I found disability both an attractive identity and a compelling theoretical move, whereas aging, by contrast, had never entered my theoretical ambitions?

Riva Lehrer, one of my favorite crip theorists, offers a glimpse of an answer to this question. I previously quoted Lehrer to exemplify the attraction of "crip"; here is a longer version of the same passage: "Old women disappear into a slow molasses of obscurity, even when they fight to be seen. I can see the day coming when the shape of my body will be chalked up to age and I will join the ranks of the Invisible Women. *Until then*, I will be one of the crip girls whose bodies scare the panel of judges. They are afraid that our unbalanced shapes hint of unsanctioned desires."[15]

I emphasize Lehrer's "until then" because it marks the divide between disability and aging. When Lehrer's disability is "chalked up to age," it will no longer "hint of unsanctioned desires." Her extraordinary body will devolve from scary, antinormative, hypervisible, and queer to invisible and desexualized. "Then," she will *no longer be* "one of the crip girls." The combination of disability and age threatens to undo the queerness of disability.

This move from crip to aging is not just a personal problem, not just an identity crisis, but a question of discursive fields and theoretical frames. My own preference for disability over aging as intellectual framework was, I came to realize, typical of the entire field of queer theory. While disability studies has generated much lively queer theory and vice versa, there is virtually no work at the intersection of queer theory and aging. According to Barbara Marshall and Stephen Katz, sociologists who study sexuality and aging, "theoretical and historical inquiries that address the different cultures and discourses in which age and sex figure prominently . . . generally fail to consider their areas of intersection."[16]

Although a number of queer theorists have written about adolescents and children, I know of no queer theorists who have looked at adult aging. Recently, however, a few scholars of aging have made connections between old age and queer. One of the earliest of these is Linn Sandberg's 2008 article "The Old, the Ugly and the Queer." Despite old age being "little discussed . . . within queer theory," Sandberg asserts that "age holds great potential for how to rethink sexualities, gender and embodiment."[17] I would like to think that the present book might flesh out Sandberg's bold assertion.

While Sandberg's article was published in a little-known journal for graduate student writing, three years later, Gullette's well-received book *Agewise* has a chapter on sexuality that builds to this rousing conclusion: "Later-life sexualities radically spoken have big things to teach. . . . Just believing there are thousands of different long-term sexual narratives out there might mean less current suffering . . . more liberty. . . . Queering the whole sexual life course we might call it, because it seems a more radical kind of sexual revolution than history has known."[18]

Gullette had already published three major books on aging, but this 2011 book is not only the first with a chapter devoted to sexuality; it is the first time she makes any reference to "queer." Gullette here associates "later-life sexualities" with queer, a connection reflected in terms like "radical . . . sexual revolution" and in the plural of "sexualities." This link between later-life sexualities and queer is absolutely central to the present book.

Beyond the general connection to queer here, Gullette's phrase "queering the whole sexual life course" can also link to what by the time of her 2011 book was the most prominent trend in queer theory, what I will here refer to as "queer temporality." In the twenty-first century, a range of queer theorists have brought the resistance to normativity and the valuation of alternative lives that characterize queer theory to bear on various aspects of temporality.[19] While no queer theorist that I know of has used the phrase "life course," this phrase appears when Sandberg's 2008 article advocates for the application of "queer temporalities" to old age: "Pre-given and naturalized moral codes of old age may be challenged through queer temporalities revealing the constructed nature of the life course."[20]

Although Sandberg is, to my knowledge, the first to suggest the applicability of queer temporality to aging, her article touches on the topic only briefly. A year later, however, Maria T. Brown, a lesbian gerontologist, gives queer temporality much more extensive consideration, and the "life course" features prominently in her account. Brown discusses the work of two major figures in queer temporality, Judith (Jack) Halberstam and Elizabeth Freeman. "In terms of gerontological theory," Brown writes, "Halberstam is stating that queer time falls outside of and rejects the institutionalized life course. . . . Both Freeman and Halberstam have rejected . . . the institutionalized life course in favor of making visible the many alternative kinds of lives and temporal orders of possible life events."[21] Brown translates queer temporality into the "terms of gerontological theory": central to that translation is the idea of the "life course," a concept from the social sciences important for those studying aging. A life course is "a sequence of socially defined events and roles that the individual enacts over time."[22] Using "institutionalized" for what queer theorists would call normative, Brown understands queer time theory as a rejection of the normative life course in favor of alternative, nonnormative, temporal orderings of life. With the help of Brown's translation, we can see that the goal of queer temporality is indeed what we might call, following Gullette, queering the life course.

Brown recognizes what gerontological theory would call the institutionalized life course in what Halberstam calls "the paradigmatic markers of life experience—namely, birth, marriage, reproduction, and death."[23] It is in particular the place of marriage and reproduction on this list of "paradigmatic markers" that queer temporality contests, challenging the sexual life course that privileges reproduction and devalues nonreproductive lives and moments. The addition of a temporal dimension to the queer critique of reproductivity could mean not just the reclaiming of queer lives outside of marriage-and-children but also the reclaiming of nonreproductive moments like postmenopausal sexuality. Queering the life course means contesting the temporal order that dictates which segments of life are properly sexual and which are not.

Although Brown establishes the terms for applying queer temporality to aging, her response to this trend in queer theory is in fact mainly disappointment: theorists like Halberstam and Freeman may want to "make visible" alternative kinds of lives, but their conceptions of queer time "make invisible" the experience of aging.[24] Whereas Brown's account of queer time was largely critical of the theory's neglect of old people, in 2012, Cynthia Port, one of the editors of the journal *Age, Culture, Humanities*, explicitly embraced queer temporality as a resource for the study of old age: "Although there are significant differences between queer sexuality and old age as embodied subjectivities and categories of identity, these new approaches to queer temporality suggest intriguing possibilities for reconsidering the temporalities of old age."[25]

While I certainly share Brown's sense that queer temporality theory has neglected old age, I nonetheless heartily endorse Port's appreciation of this theory as a valuable resource for thinking about aging. In fact, soon after realizing I needed to add aging to the intersectional focus of this book, I began to imagine thinking queer temporality and aging together. Just as crip theory makes it possible to think disability through queer, this second theoretical intersection could allow this book to queer aging.

Before I began working on this book, before I began reading extensively in crip theory, I was in fact working on and with "queer temporality." I took the phrase from a 2002 article by Stephen M. Barber and David L. Clark on temporality in the work of Eve Sedgwick, which is, I believe, the earliest example of what grew into a major trend in queer theory.[26] In my last book, I used queer temporality to talk about writing and death, and following Sedgwick, I stressed that queer was a twisted temporality, not linear or straight, focusing on moments that were out of order.[27] This interest in twisted temporality persists in the present book, applying in particular to moments when sexuality puts a kink in normative time lines and narrative arcs.

Because I had thus been immersed in queer temporality theory, it was perhaps inevitably the viewpoint from which I would consider aging, since aging is, as Gullette says, what we call a "form of temporality."[28] Indeed I would say that aging is all about temporality, is literally the lived experience of temporality. To add aging to our analysis is not so much to add another identity group as to add temporality to our crip theory, to add temporality to our understandings of sexuality and the body.

As I was contemplating using queer temporality to think about aging, I was very happy to read Port's 2012 article, happy to find someone in age studies who believed this could be a productive theoretical intersection.[29] Like Brown, Port cites Halberstam and Freeman, but the queer theory Port finds most useful makes no appearance in Brown's article. Port titles her article "No Future?"—which refers to Lee Edelman's controversial and influential 2004 book *No Future*.

While Halberstam's and Freeman's understandings of queer time are rooted in queer culture, Edelman's temporality theory is rooted in what queers represent in the view of the normative social order. According to Edelman, normative temporality is a compulsory futurism (subordinating everything to the promise of the future), and queers represent a threat to the social order's compulsory preference for the future over the present.[30] It is this formulation that Port applies quite effectively to the old: "The old are often, like queers, figured by the cultural imagination as being outside mainstream temporalities and standing in the way of, rather than contributing to, the promise of the future."[31]

Edelman connects futurism to reproductivity; in *No Future*, the privileged figure for the promise of the future is the Child (with a capital C to suggest its sacred status). By practicing nonreproductive sexuality, queers pursue sexuality not imbued with the possibility of leading to the Child, not redeemed by the promise of the future. Though it is not Edelman's explicit concern, this privileging of the future and the Child can certainly be connected to the devaluing and desexualizing of people past their childbearing years.

Edelman's book has been both influential and controversial because of its aggressive, unyielding stance, often characterized as "antisocial." While Edelman's work does not play a central role in the present book, I would love to bring its edgy militancy into my challenge to normative aging. *No Future* urges queers to take up our place as threats to the Child and to the future. In the time since *No Future* was published, more and more openly gay people are entering the institutionalized life course, getting married and having children. On this particular point, the American cultural imagination has changed so quickly that queer may no longer figure as the threat it was as recently as 2004. In the current moment, the worship of the reproductive future might in fact devalue old people even more than it does queers. Perhaps that is what Gullette means when she says that asserting later-life sexualities may lead to "a more radical kind of sexual revolution than history has known."[32]

If *No Future* is Port's most important influence from queer theory, her central influence from aging studies is in fact Gullette's work on decline. Gullette's decline theory is likewise central to the present book's attempt to connect queer temporality to aging. Over the course of two wonderful books—*Declining to Decline* in 1997 and *Aged by Culture* in 2004—Gullette lays out her conceptualization of the temporal arc that dominates our ideas of adult aging.[33] Port refers to this as "decline ideology"; Gullette, grounded in literary temporality, more often calls it "the decline story." According to Port, it is "a narrative structure that associates old age with inevitable decline."[34] Introducing it in 1997, Gullette calls it a "Master Narrative of the Life Course."[35] Gullette's theory of decline names and elucidates a major normative temporality, the temporality that dominates our understandings and apprehensions of the second half of the life course, of aging into the middle years and beyond.

I share Port's sense that Gullette's theory works well in conjunction with queer temporality.[36] Gullette outlines and critiques the normative life course in which a person enters into decline after the age of reproduction, and that certainly accords with the queer critique of the devaluing of nonreproductive lives and moments. In her life and in her work, Gullette devotes herself to "declining to decline," to resisting the cultural dominance of the decline story. Such resistance to normative temporality is a stance also taken by the various proponents of queer temporality.

Gullette's decline theory is, however, crucial to the present book not just because of its aptitude for queer temporality. It is utterly central to this book because it can work with both queer theory and crip theory. Gullette has given us a theory of aging that implicates not just sexuality but also, and perhaps more so, disability.

Declining to Decline fleshes out the concept of the decline story by telling about the debilitating back pain that befell Gullette at age forty-nine. She goes to a doctor who pronounces, "You can't do the things you did when you were young"; the patient hears that, imagines a future of progressive decline, and is "plunged into planning [her] suicide."[37] *Declining to Decline* teaches us that such moments of entrance into catastrophic loss typify our culture's construction of aging.

This story is a good example of the present book's particular focus: a disability whose onset arises in midlife, an experience that can be equally understood as either disability or aging, although Gullette understands this experience through the latter rubric. The connection to disability is not, however, just in her personal story; it is also in her general theory of decline. What Gullette calls the decline story is in fact the insistent entanglement of loss of youth with disability.

The "master narrative" that Gullette has identified actually applies as well to our normative understandings and apprehensions of disability that befalls adults. If no one has yet applied Gullette's theory of decline to disability, it may be because we have not thought disability enough in relation to temporality. Disability tends to be thought of as a lifelong identity category; we have generally not considered crip temporalities, have not reflected enough on ways bodies change over time.[38] To add temporality to crip theory, and to focus as we do here on the particular temporality of late-onset disability, is to find Gullette's theorizing an absolutely crucial resource.

Approaching this intersection from the other direction, crip theory has a lot to offer the analysis of aging—in particular, its militant resistance to the privileging of the normative body. For example, as mentioned earlier in this introduction, Tom Shakespeare, in an article from 2000, suggests that "disabled people can challenge the obsession with fitness and youth" that characterizes our culture.[39] A thorough consideration of aging, an integration into our analyses of the fact that all bodies change over the life course, can open up crip theory to relevance for everybody who fears that aging will mean a decline into disability.

The present book uses crip theory to resist the decline story, because what Gullette calls the decline story, which dominates our fears and responses to adult aging, is not only based in the cultural privileging of "fitness and youth"; it is ultimately based in the assumption of the inferior humanity of the disabled.

That assumption of inferior humanity is also an assumption of inferior sexuality. A crip perspective is perhaps particularly useful for attending to and valuing later-life sexualities. "Aging populations," writes Emily Wentzell, "face similar issues in the realm of sexuality as disabled individuals; they are presumed to be asexual, their sexual expression is discouraged, and their physical expressions of sexuality may be devalued."[40] Wentzell, one of the very few scholars familiar with both disability and aging studies, proposes that we apply crip theory to the sexual issues of old people.

The present book focuses on a range of experiences that can be understood as either disability or aging, what I here call late-onset disability. The particular concern of this book is how late-onset disability is lived sexually: how it is lived as a threat to one's sexuality and to one's gender, but also how sexuality survives and transforms in the process, a sexuality becoming, in these older, less able subjects, more perverse from a normative (ageist, ableist) standpoint. Taking its antinormative audacity from queer and especially crip theory, this book explores and celebrates the perverse sexuality of the no longer young, no longer so able.

Aging and the Phallus

The "phallus" in this book's subtitle is the aspect of the book that I have consistently found the most embarrassing. When friends or colleagues ask what I am working on, as they so often do, I easily and proudly say "a book on sexuality, disability, and aging," but I almost never tell anyone that the book is also about the phallus. In fact, I often wish I could excise this aspect.

The phallus here is a psychoanalytic concept. It derives from my decades of familiarity with Freudian and Lacanian psychoanalytic theory. I did not, in fact, set out to write a book about the phallus, but as I progressed into this work on the intersection of sexuality, disability, and aging, I was surprised to find this concept suggesting itself, persistently and insistently. Over the years I worked on this book, I came to believe that the notion of the phallus (denatured by three decades of queer theory) has a substantial contribution to make to our theorization of sexuality as lived in and over time.

I find this not only embarrassing but also ironic. Throughout the 1970s and 1980s, I wrote about psychoanalysis from a feminist point of view. And while I found psychoanalysis invaluable as an antinormative theory of sexuality, my writing over those two decades was consistently critical of the dominance of the phallus in psychoanalytic theory. For example, in 1980 I wrote, "It is the rule of the Phallus as standard for any sexuality which denigrates women."[41] As someone who contributed to the feminist critique of the psychoanalytic concept of the phallus, I feel sheepish indeed to return here to the phallus as a term for thinking about sexuality.

The relation between the psychoanalytic phallus and androcentrism has in fact been the subject of debate for nearly a century now.[42] There have been cogent and persuasive arguments made on both sides. One can convincingly argue both that the phallus is a fatally androcentric concept and that it is not. In psychoanalysis, the phallus is not the penis. As Lacan puts it, "Clinical facts . . . reveal a relation of the subject to the phallus that is established without regard to the anatomical difference of the sexes."[43] On the other hand, as I myself argued in the 1980s, the phallus cannot simply be separated from its association with the penis, however much psychoanalytic theory would like to make that separation.[44]

Having taken up the phallus again in this book, I find myself once again ensnared in this debate. Whenever I have presented material from this book, while the audience is generally enthusiastic, I always get a question about the androcentrism of the term "phallus." And I always find myself unable to answer to either my questioner's or my own satisfaction. I wish I could definitively prove that the phallus was not male centered, or I wish I could find a better, more gender-neutral term for what I am talking about in this book. But, at least for now, I am stuck with the phallus, and with its sexist baggage.

The phallus might not even be the worst of the terms I am here getting from psychoanalysis. That dubious honor probably goes to the phallus's polar opposite. In the most sexist understanding of psychoanalytic theory, women are considered "castrated." In this formulation, women not only do not have the phallus; they are devoid of any sexuality, simply lacking, empty. Despite this unsavory association, I in fact regularly use the concept of castration in this book.

Both late-onset disability and aging are experienced as threats to one's sexuality and to one's gender (regardless of the gender with which one identifies). This sense of impending loss, a loss tangling together gender and sexuality, can best be understood, I propose, as a form of castration anxiety. Yet, despite its centrality to my argument here, I continue to feel squeamish about the term "castration." Which is why I am heartened to find it in the writings of two of my favorite theorists of aging.

Kathleen Woodward was a pioneering advocate for age studies in the humanities and for decades has been a major figure in the field; she is also well versed in psychoanalytic theory. Her 1991 book, *Aging and Its Discontents*, looks at aging from a psychoanalytic perspective. "Old age," writes Woodward, "in Freudian terms is castration."[45] Although Woodward admits that her book does not focus much on sexuality, this recognition of the relevance of Freudian castration to old age is crucial for my present attempt to think sexuality and aging together.[46]

I am grateful to Woodward for applying a psychoanalytic perspective to adult aging. "Lacan has insisted," Woodward writes, "that the 'fear of castration is like a thread that perforates all the stages of development.'"[47] When we think of "stages of development," especially in relation to psychoanalysis, we think of stages on the way to adulthood. But after quoting Lacan on the presence of the fear of castration in *all the stages* of development, Woodward proceeds to elaborate on our "anxieties about aging in middle age": "Does not identification in middle age with a parent in an infirm old age represent precisely . . . future castration[?] . . . In an infirm old age the body of the father embodies the very fact of castration."[48]

The Freudian perspective here is recognizable in notions like "identification with a parent," although the figure identifying with a parent is not a child but a middle-aged person. The phrase "fact of castration" can be found in Freud's writings (as well as other psychoanalytic theory) and has been roundly criticized by feminists (myself included) since castration is not a fact but a surmise. Yet while Freud uses "fact of castration" to refer to women, Woodward redeploys Freud's phrase to refer to old men (to fathers, no less). Woodward's idea that the body of the old father "embodies the very fact of castration" depends on and reinforces a dramatic differentiation between penis and phallus. Her book in fact begins by discussing a photograph of a naked old man, "sitting . . . , his knees wide apart, . . . his alcoholic stomach . . . as slack as his penis. His entire body seemed to be hanging down, depressed."[49] This old man's body, complete with visible penis, represents the very opposite of the phallus, "embodies the very fact of castration."

In Woodward's elaboration on old age as figuring castration, I would also note her repetition of the phrase "infirm old age." The image of aging as castration here cannot be separated from an image of infirmity. Not only does Woodward's representation of castration thus reinforce the theoretical conjoining of aging and disability in the present book, but it also intimates our focus here on castration as a temporality of the phallus.

The phrase "future castration" in the passage from Woodward's book suggests that the middle-aged person contemplating his (or her) infirm old parent anxiously beholds a scenario in which his (or her) present phallus will sometime in the future be lost. Yet "future" is not the only temporal marker in this passage. The phrase "the fact of castration," the very use of the psychoanalytic notion of castration, suggests that sometime in the past this old father was phallic but then lost his phallus. Castration, as used by psychoanalysis, is itself an inherently temporal notion in that it configures *whoever does not have the phallus as having had it in the past.*

This sense of castration as a temporal notion is at the center of the present book. Whereas castration's inherent temporality makes it a dubious fit for representing gender difference, it may make the notion particularly apt as a way of talking about age. What Woodward sketches for us in the middle-aged person's contemplation of infirm old age is what in this book I term the "classic temporality of the phallus"—here, however, distributed not on the basis of gender, but on the basis of age. The classic temporality of the phallus is one where those who are "castrated" were phallic in the past (in Freud, women; in Woodward, the infirm old) and those who are phallic fear "future castration" (in Freud, men; in Woodward, the middle-aged).

While Woodward's topic is aging and old age generally, she locates castration anxiety specifically in middle age. In so doing, she makes reference to the premier theorist of middle age, Margaret Morganroth Gullette.[50] While Gullette is much more ambivalent about the use of psychoanalytic theory than is Woodward, the concept of castration does appear, sporadically, across her work.

In the book Woodward refers to, *Safe at Last in the Middle Years*, castration appears via a John Updike character. Published in 1988, *Safe at Last* is the first of Gullette's books on aging, and it is much more based in literary criticism than are the later books. Gullette begins the first chapter of *Safe at Last* by talking about trouble with teeth in midlife novels, which leads her to the dentist in Updike's *Couples* who declares: "Losing a tooth . . . is a classic castration symbol." Gullette goes on to comment: "The limp, castration-concerned dentist gets to enunciate the decline theory of life."[51]

While we would not want to confuse Gullette's point of view with that of Updike's dentist, it is worth noting that in her comment about him, she connects castration with the decline theory. This is the first mention in the first chapter of her first book of what will become her major contribution to the theorization of aging. Her next book is titled *Declining to Decline*, and her work henceforth is focused on identifying and resisting what she here calls the decline theory of life. Because my project involves connecting Gullette's decline theory with the psychoanalytic notion of castration, I am happy to see that, early in her formulation of the decline theory, she herself makes that connection, if only tangentially, anecdotally.

Gullette's later references to the Freudian castration complex, while all definitely fleeting, are more substantively connected to her theorizing, rather than to the point of view of a fictional character. In an article published in 1998, for example, while discussing a change that occurred in the relative valuation of younger and older men in the early twentieth century, Gullette writes: "'Penis envy,' which Freud named but misidentified, became a problem for older men."[52] In the Freudian schema, penis envy is what those who are castrated feel toward those who are not. While Woodward focused on the fear of castration that the younger man feels contemplating the older man, Gullette reverses that gaze and attributes penis envy to the older man.

From a feminist perspective, penis envy is probably the most offensive aspect of the Freudian castration complex, even more so than castration anxiety. Freud's use of "penis" in the phrase makes this aspect of the castration complex harder to defend, unsuitable for the usual tactic of separating phallus from penis. Well aware of the feminist distaste for the term, Gullette suggests that while penis envy is mistaken as a way of understanding women, it could be useful as a way of understanding older men's relation to younger men.

In her 2011 book, *Agewise*, Gullette brings up the Freudian concept of castration in a discussion of menopause: "For those who accept the theory of menopause as an endocrine deficiency, it functions somewhat as the Freudian concept of female castration used to do, except it comes later in life. The universal menopause represents women as suddenly damaged and desexualized bodies."[53] Here again Gullette cites the Freudian concept while also taking distance from it. For her, as for most of us feminists, female castration is an outmoded concept ("functions . . . as the Freudian concept of female castration *used to do*"). Yet, while marking her distance from this objectionable concept, she also finds it useful, in the context of her critique of ageism.

"Castration," as Gullette uses it here, means not the loss of a male sexual organ, but "suddenly damaged and desexualized bodies." That definition is very much the operative one in the present book. I thus want to note a couple things about Gullette's definition of castration. By connecting "desexualized" to "damaged bodies," she gestures toward the intersection of disability and sexuality central to my deployment of crip theory. And Gullette's "suddenly" points to an insistent temporal dimension in the concept of castration. In the drama of castration, damage and desexualization occur to the body not as a process over time, but as a traumatic event, changing everything in a moment.

Although Gullette's use of castration here would seem to apply specifically to women, it nonetheless jibes with Woodward's image of castration. Woodward's example is definitely male (the old father's body), but she also uses the gender-neutral terms "parent" and "child." While Gullette's example is menopause, she goes on to say that this "later in life" castration applies to men, too.[54] In both authors, castration is connected to gender and yet also seems to apply without regard to gender. This contradictory relation to gender indeed seems to inhere in the psychoanalytic concept of castration.

In both Woodward's and Gullette's usages, castration threatens those in middle age. The use of the term by these two pioneering and widely influential age theorists, especially taken together, reinforces my belief that castration is a pertinent concept for understanding the projections connected to ageism and the anxieties connected to aging. Let me be clear: neither Woodward nor Gullette is saying that old people are castrated; nor am I. But we all have noted that castration, as delineated by Freud (however mistaken it might be), functions in our apprehensions around aging. The specific temporality of castration anxiety—the scenario of a future losing it once-and-for-all—is the prospect we find over and over in midlife aging (and also in relation to late-onset disability).

In this book, I consider castration anxiety as a "temporality of the phallus." In this anxious scenario, the phallus is an inescapably temporal concept: if present, it threatens to disappear suddenly in the future; if absent, the assumption is that it was once present but was traumatically excised in some past moment. This is the classic temporality of the phallus, present in every psychoanalytic account of the phallus and castration. I consider this temporality to be normative.

In addition to outlining the normative temporality of the phallus, I track alternative temporalities of the phallus, where one might move *from* castration *to* phallus as well as in the other direction, where the lost phallus is surprisingly regained, or where the phallus might appear not only in the past but as a promising future. These alternatives echo the promises of queer temporality and may lead to less-anxious castrations and queerer phalluses.

The Queer Phallus

The queer phallus is a somewhat hazy, possibly dubious, idea circulating in or around the discourse of queer theory over the past two decades. While never, to my knowledge, clarified or affirmed, it nonetheless persists. And this queer phallus, whatever it might mean, whether or not it exists, has a role to play in this book, whether as theoretical concept or perhaps as the book's obscure object of desire. The phallus, Lacan has said, "can play its role only when veiled."[55] That seems at the least to be true of this "queer phallus."

Perhaps the most substantive appearance of the queer phallus is in a book by Jan Campbell, published in 2000, that includes a chapter titled "Queering the Phallus." This chapter title speaks to me since my goal here is not to posit the queer phallus per se, but to queer the phallus, to denature and denormativize the phallus and its temporalities. "Queer theory," according to Campbell, "tak[es] Freud's theory of the phallus and reinvent[s] it in a more positive understanding of female or lesbian desire."[56]

While Campbell's phrasing suggests a general use of the phallus in queer theory, she in fact adduces only two examples of theorists who queer the phallus: Teresa de Lauretis in 1994 and Judith Butler in 1993.[57] These examples are, admittedly, pretty high-profile figures in queer theory (especially as it appeared in the 1990s). Butler's work is widely recognized as formative for the queer theory that arose in the early 1990s, and de Lauretis is often credited with originating the phrase "queer theory."[58]

Butler and de Lauretis were not in fact talking about a "queer" phallus; what was at stake for both theorists was a "lesbian" phallus. Versed in psychoanalytic theory, both de Lauretis and Butler in the early 1990s argued for something like a phallus in lesbian desire and sexual practice.[59] Based on the psychoanalytic distinction between phallus and penis, they point to the operation of the phallus in this sexuality without a penis.

Butler comes right out and puts "the lesbian phallus" in the very title of her essay. De Lauretis, on the other hand, though she takes a position similar to Butler's, stops short of endorsing the word "phallus." De Lauretis declares that a "notion of castration and *some* notion of the phallus—some notion of signifier of desire—are necessary to understand the processes and forms of subjectivity." De Lauretis italicizes the word "some" in the phrase "*some* notion of the phallus," suggesting a question about which notion of the phallus she will use. She then goes on to say that "Judith Butler proposes . . . 'the lesbian Phallus,'" but notes, "I prefer to call the signifier of perverse desire a *fetish*."[60]

Allowing that *some* notion of the phallus is necessary, in contradistinction to Butler, de Lauretis prefers the term "fetish," "in order to avoid the unavoidable semantic complicity of phallus with penis, even at the risk of evoking the negative (reductive) connotations that the term *fetish* also currently carries." The phallus, for de Lauretis, is a "signifier of desire," but when she wants a "signifier of perverse desire"—that is, a queer phallus—she prefers not to use the term "phallus" because it cannot be separated from penis. Instead she uses "fetish," another psychoanalytic term, despite her awareness that this term has its own drawbacks. I share de Lauretis's desire for a phallic signifier that can "avoid the unavoidable semantic complicity" with penis, but unlike her I don't believe "fetish" can solve the problem—especially when I see that by 2000, Campbell assimilates de Lauretis's lesbian fetish back into the general category of the (queer) phallus.

If we were to respect de Lauretis's preference for not using the term "phallus," we would then be left with really only one example of queering the phallus: Judith Butler's essay "The Lesbian Phallus and the Morphological Imaginary." It is odd to think of one essay as representing an entire trend in queer theory. But Butler's essay does have a pretty interesting profile, both in Campbell's account and in queer discourse more generally.

According to Campbell, Butler "does not leave the phallocentric discourse of psychoanalysis behind; instead she performs it differently."[61] While Butler is indeed known for bringing notions of performance and performativity to psychoanalytic theory, Campbell seems here to be talking not about Butler's theory of performance, but about her performance of theory, about how she performs phallocentric psychoanalysis. It is in light of this statement about Butler's performing that I remark that Campbell's chapter has a section titled "Butler's Performing Phallus" and that this section opens with the phrase "Judith Butler's famous lesbian phallus." The idea of fame resonates with the idea of performance here.

Campbell concludes her discussion of Butler's essay expressing doubt and asking a question: "Butler's notion of a mobile lesbian phallus remains problematic. If the sign of the phallus is so mobile that it can symbolize lesbian bodily parts, then why still call it the phallus?"[62] Campbell's account of Butler's essay thus ultimately comes back to the perennial objection to using the male-centered term "phallus," but this unavoidable logical objection coexists with a playful, admiring response to Butler's performance, to her "performing phallus." Not just in Campbell's account but more generally, I would say that the response to Butler's essay combines persuasive logical objection to the concept with enthusiasm for the performance of the "famous lesbian phallus." Based on over twenty years of response, I would say that Butler's lesbian phallus seems to be both wrong and thrilling.

More than a decade after Campbell's "Queering the Phallus," Lili Hsieh proposes to "query the queering of the Phallus . . . by queer feminists."[63] "Isn't it time," Hsieh's article begins by asking, "to sweep the 'Empire of the Phallus' . . . into the dustbin of history?"[64] This rhetorical question suggests that what Hsieh calls "queering phallus" was still in 2012 a flourishing theoretical direction in need of critique.[65] "Queering phallus" is here exemplified by Butler's essay.

Mounting a knowledgeable and attentive critique of Butler's use of the term "phallus," Hsieh refers to "her celebrated concept of the 'lesbian phallus.'"[66] "Celebrated" here recalls Campbell's "famous," but it also connotes twenty years of enthusiastic reception for Butler's concept. To exemplify that reception, Hsieh cites a 2010 blog post by Tavia Nyong'o: "Judith Butler is 'pulling the strings of the nation's impressionable youth through film and video' because . . . Lady Gaga is showing us her lesbian phallus."[67] This connection to Lady Gaga (not to mention "film and video" and "impressionable youth") provides perhaps the perfect instantiation for the fame/performance nexus that Campbell attached a dozen years earlier to the lesbian phallus.

There is something about Butler's "lesbian phallus" essay that, despite its meticulous close work with Freudian and Lacanian theory, operates as brazen, ballsy performance. This essay may in fact be Butler's most playful; there seems to be something seductive going on. Perhaps because the idea of a lesbian phallus is so desirable, so titillating to readers—or maybe it's just me.[68]

"The Lesbian Phallus" opens: "After such a promising title, I knew that I could not possibly offer a satisfying essay." This opening presumes her readers want to hear about the lesbian phallus, that we are eager to get what she is promising us, that the phrase "the lesbian phallus" provokes desire. The first paragraph goes on to talk not just about "the promise of the phallus" but also about its "allure": "Perhaps a certain wariness with respect to that allure is a good thing."[69] The phallus according to Butler: alluring, so beware.

Butler bases her contribution to the theorization of the phallus on Lacan's assertion that the phallus is not the penis. She then goes on to posit that the phallus is displaceable, that "the phallus can attach to a variety of organs," and beyond that, to "other body-like things." The "displaceability of the phallus," writes Butler, "opens the way for the lesbian phallus."[70] While she carefully shows that the phallus in Lacan is displaceable, transferable, mobile, her close textual work with psychoanalytic theory merely "opens the way" for the lesbian phallus; it does not get us there. "The lesbian phallus," she writes, "may be said to intervene as an unexpected consequence of the Lacanian scheme."[71] *Intervene, unexpected*: the lesbian phallus is an intruder in the Lacanian scheme, an interloper in the psychoanalytic theorization of the phallus.

The move to the lesbian phallus, although carefully prepared through a reading of Lacanian theory, ultimately occurs by gesturing toward lesbian sexual practice. For example, "'having' the phallus can be symbolized by an arm, a tongue, a hand (or two), a knee, a thigh, a pelvic bone, an array of purposefully instrumentalized body-like things."[72] This list intimates a repertoire of ways someone without a penis might "satisfy" a woman, might give sexual pleasure to a woman.[73] The parenthetic "(or two)" is a playful, knowing wink. Not only does Butler's lesbian phallus intervene where not expected, but it then proceeds to flaunt its familiarity with the ways of pleasuring a woman, operating its lesbian seduction.

In a less playful tone, however, the essay insistently marks the lesbian phallus as wrong. For example, Butler reminds us that "the phallus is . . . excommunicated from the feminist orthodoxy on lesbian sexuality."[74] The lesbian phallus, the essay goes on to say, is doubly prohibited, both by misogyny and by feminism, both by heterosexism and by lesbian discourse. Under all this prohibition, the lesbian phallus cannot help but be "a source of shame."[75] Butler's delineation of the shame attached to the phallus she brings forth, as I reread it now, sets me to thinking of my own embarrassment at the phallus in the present book's title.

Even as she advances the lesbian phallus, Butler makes clear that it is unavoidably wrong, in a number of different ways. Yet it remains nonetheless bold and thrilling, a promise of pleasure and of alternative sexual theorizing, "the production of an anti-heterosexist sexual imaginary."[76] It is the insistence of its promise along with the persistence of its wrongness that makes Butler's lesbian phallus particularly "queer." This is the sort of queer phallus, wrong but nonetheless alluring, sexy and incorrect, which is at play in the present book, in my use of the phallus here.

Butler's phallus is wrong, queer, because it is lesbian, because it belongs to someone who does not have a penis. As such, its inappropriateness belongs to the nearly century-long critique of how psychoanalysis applies the term "phallus" to women's sexuality as well as to men's. But I would like here to gesture toward an even broader queerness, a more generally inappropriate phallus.

In her 2012 article, Hsieh writes: "Lacan chooses the unfortunate signifier of the phallus. . . . The phallus is a misnomer of something larger that lurks in human sexuality."[77] For Hsieh, it is not just Butler's lesbian phallus but Lacan's phallus that is wrong. "Unfortunate signifier," "misnomer": Lacan is wrong to choose the word "phallus." The Lacanian phallus is not just wrong for women; it is wrong for everyone.

Yet unlike de Lauretis, who proposed we replace it with "fetish," Hsieh does not propose a more "fortunate signifier" to replace phallus. She does not offer a correct name for this "misnomer"; she proffers instead the phrase "something larger that lurks in human sexuality." I like this evocative phrase. There does seem to be an insistent connection between the phallus and "something larger." The verb "lurks" suggests the shady, inappropriate, threatening side, as well as the veiled nature, of the phallus's operation. And the entire phrase implies that we cannot identify it, don't know exactly what it is, although we do know it is connected to sexuality, and it is larger.

While I thoroughly agree with Hsieh that "phallus" is an unfortunate signifier, I cannot get beyond the misnomer here, cannot do without this word. The phallus in the present book is a misnomer for something we don't (yet) have a correct name for. The phallus in this book is queer that way.

Anecdotal Theory

Before I bring this introduction to a close, a few comments about a particular aspect of the book's methodology are in order. The book that follows is made up of two chapters, both of which begin with a short personal narrative that I wrote especially for this book. The first chapter opens with an account of problems with my feet and walking that arose as I approached the age of fifty. The second chapter includes a brief chronicle of sexual activity and attitudes during a two-year period starting when my partner was diagnosed with prostate cancer. This personal writing functions here as catalyst and focus for an extended critical and theoretical inquiry, delving into related issues and texts. This procedure, starting from personal narrative in order to theorize, is something I have called, in an earlier book, "anecdotal theory."

As that 2002 book explains, during the 1990s "I experimented with writing in which I would recount an anecdote and then attempt to 'read' that account for the theoretical insights it afforded."[78] When I collected those experiments together in one volume, it was this particular practice, this method of theorizing, that I wanted to indicate by the title *Anecdotal Theory*. While that book focused on pedagogy, feminism, and the academy, this book, despite having decidedly different theoretical concerns, shares its methodology.

The idea of combining personal writing with theoretical inquiry came to me, first of all, from feminist studies. Since the beginning of the movement for women's studies, feminist academics have criticized the way a certain professionalization of knowledge denied connections between knowledge and the world. Feminist epistemology emphasized the value of revealing the concrete conditions that produce knowledge. The inclusion of the personal within the scholarly was seen by some of the pioneers of academic feminism as a way to consider thoughts, responses, and insights that would not traditionally be recognized as knowledge.

Through the 1980s and 1990s, more and more feminist scholars began "doing theory," incorporating poststructuralist theory into their feminist work. While some thought this would mean the end of personal scholarly writing, I was far from the only feminist at that time bringing personal writing into our theory. In her study of academic feminist memoirs of the 1990s, Cynthia Franklin in fact notes there was a movement "to combine personal experience and theory."[79] While often critical of 1990s academic memoirs, especially personal writing seen as a retreat from theory, Franklin applauds writing that combines memoir with theory, praising books that "successfully bring personal narrative and theory into a dialectical relationship."[80] Franklin values memoir for what it can add to theory: "Personal writing can address complexities and contradictions that escape even the most nuanced theoretical formulations."[81]

While feminist thought was decisive in my turn to "combine personal experience and theory," there is also a second crucial theoretical influence on those 1990s essays of mine: the experiment derives not just from feminism but also from psychoanalysis. Proclaiming that "psychoanalysis is an anecdotal theory," my 2002 book went on to explain that "by grounding theory in case history, psychoanalysis demands that theory test itself against the uncanny details of story."[82] This may be what I most value about what I call anecdotal theory: that by beginning in case history, theorizing must honor and answer to the detail of lived experience.

The psychoanalytic background to anecdotal theory is not, however, just about the relation between theory and case history; it is also about sex. My 1990s essays and the present book, despite their broad divergence in topic, share a focus on sexuality. *Anecdotal Theory* was concerned with pedagogy, whereas this book addresses disability and aging, but both writing projects locate themselves in an exploration of how their particular topics are lived sexually. In both books, the memoir component is not just personal but specifically sexual.

My 2002 book articulates some of the goals of anecdotal theory thus: "Rather than reach a general understanding via the norm, I choose to theorize via a . . . marginal case. I'm trying to theorize . . . in a way that resists the norm. . . . The usual presupposition of theory is that we need to reach a general understanding, which then predisposes us toward the norm, toward a case or model that is prevalent, mainstream. To dismiss something as 'merely anecdotal' is to dismiss it as a . . . marginal case."[83]

Psychoanalysis can be this sort of anecdotal theory as well;[84] psychoanalytic thinking can participate in this resistance to the norm. Freud theorized sexuality based on perversions rather than the reproductive norm. This Freudian understanding of sexuality challenged the reigning model of sexuality as defined by reproductive teleology, a model that would restrict sexuality to acts and people capable of biological reproduction.[85] Not only did Freud define sexuality so as to include in its crux practices defined as perverse (by not being reproductive), but he more famously expanded it to prepubescent behavior, thus radically unseating reproductivity from its position of dominance within our understanding of sexuality. It is this antinormative heritage of psychoanalysis that I embrace for anecdotal theory.

By the time I published *Anecdotal Theory*, two things had happened to me that together would eventually lead to the present book. I had begun to understand my work as located within the field of queer theory, and I had begun to have foot pain that drastically reduced my ability to stand or walk. These two changes in my life seemed at first to have literally nothing to do with each other.

In the early 2000s I was reading extensively in queer theory. At the same time, queer theory as a field was beginning to establish connections with disability studies. My reading in queer theory led me into some radical crip theory, and sometimes I would connect to my reading not just as a queer theorist but as a crip. These brief crip reading moments occurred sporadically over a decade while my writing pursued other, less personal topics. I was no longer trying to do anecdotal theory, but every once in a while, reading at the intersection of queer and disability, I would have a fleeting fantasy of trying to theorize from my crip "standpoint."

Reading in crip theory, I rediscovered anecdotal theory. Scholarly publications at the intersection of queer theory and disability regularly included personal narrative among the theoretical work.[86] And reading those personal narratives, I would sometimes fantasize writing one myself. In the summer of 2011 I read the volume *Gay Shame* out of a theoretical interest in shame and sexuality. The book included an entire section devoted to disabled shame, and in that section was a piece of personal writing by Abby Wilkerson called "Slipping."[87] As I read Wilkerson's essay, I could not stop imagining writing up my own wheelchair story. The intensity of that urge is the origin of this book.

From the moment I read Wilkerson's "Slipping," I began obsessively composing my foot story in my head. It was two years later that I finally wrote up this account of my foot pain and how it affected my sexuality and my gender. Although I felt quite compelled to tell this story, my ultimate goal was not to write memoir, but to use that experience as a starting point to think through the relation between disability and sex.

Later, as I have already recounted in this introduction, I added aging to my theoretical agenda. Early in my attempt to catch up with critical aging studies, I read Gullette's *Declining to Decline* and discovered anecdotal theory there as well. The theorization of decline in that book begins with a chapter outlining how in midlife Gullette was overcome by serious back pain, and how that led to her grappling with decline ideology both in her life and in her theorizing.

In *Anecdotal Theory* I wrote: "While the impetus for theorizing is often the need to think through a life occurrence, the occurrence is generally not included as part of the theorizing (although it may sometimes be alluded to in prefatory material). . . . A whole lot of theory turns out to be 'anecdotal': that is, the thinking is inspired, energized, or made necessary by some puzzling, troubling, instigating life event."[88] Gullette's back pain is the "life occurrence" that instigated her theory. Unlike most theory, which relegates life event to preface or to silence, the work that I find most valuable, like Gullette's *Declining to Decline* or Eli Clare's crip classic *Exile and Pride*, includes life occurrence as more than prefatory, as part of the theorizing.[89] A lot of the theoretical work that the present book takes as inspiration, from disability and aging studies, in fact combines life writing with theory—it is not just implicitly but *explicitly* anecdotal.

In 2002, trying to explain why I did anecdotal theory, I wrote: "I theorize . . . in order better to negotiate the world in which I find myself. . . . Subjecting theory to incident teaches us to think in precisely those situations which tend to disable thought, forces us to keep thinking even when the dominance of our thought is far from assured."[90] This is a plea for the life value of theory, for theorizing as help in "negotiating the world." Although I would still subscribe to every word in this passage, rereading it now, I am quite surprised to discover the verb "disable" there. I wrote that word before I identified as disabled, wrote it actually just before the pain in my feet had become a central fact in my life. Finding it there, it seems uncanny, perhaps a prescient harbinger of the way my disability would, a decade later, make anecdotal theory newly relevant for me. Encountering it now after my immersion in crip theory, I'd like to read it as suggesting the way disability not only can threaten thought but also can at the same time teach the value of embodied thinking.

ONE

HIGH HEELS AND
WHEELCHAIRS

THE STORY

New York City and shoes: it's a long story for me. The very first time
I went to New York, I was a teenager. It was 1968; I was from Du-
luth, Minnesota, and my cousin Harvey was going to show me the
sights. Excited about seeing the big city, about my first trip alone, I
arrived wearing strappy, patent-leather sandals with heels. I wanted
to wear my most grown-up, stylish shoes for New York. After a
day of walking all over Manhattan, I counted forty-eight blisters on
my feet.

During the 1970s, as a student at Cornell, I got to New York a
lot. I remember walking and walking in the city, turned on by the
lure of window-shopping. The windows that spoke to me were filled
with gorgeous shoes, high-heeled numbers in a lush array of colors
and shapes. Whatever I wanted from New York, whatever New York
made me want, was embodied in those windows full of women's
shoes. The windows were in every neighborhood, some with out-
rageously expensive designer shoes, others full of cheap but even
sexier shoes. I don't remember if I ever actually bought a pair of
shoes in New York in the 1970s.

Over the course of the 1980s, I accumulated a lot of great shoes. I had tenure and a steady income, and shoes were my main extravagant expenditure. I remember, for example, the gold, three-inch-heel pumps; the pink-and-white-striped pumps; and the suede, high-heeled, fur-trimmed ankle boots. I remember those three pairs in particular because, although I have not been able to wear them for many years, they are still in my closet.

In the 1990s something was happening with my feet. When I had my first child in the late 1980s, it had become a little harder to find shoes that fit. After my second child in 1995, my feet got even wider; most of the shoes in my closet no longer fit. For casual everyday wear, I took to Converse Chuck Taylor All Star high-tops. They looked young and hip, and soon I had a half dozen pairs in different colors. Dress shoes were the problem: I didn't want to wear high-tops with skirts; none of the fashionable shoe stores in Milwaukee had wide-width shoes for women. New York was, in my mind, still the mecca for women's shoes. On a trip there with my partner, Dick, I found a store that catered to women with wide feet, and bought a pair of black suede, two-inch-heel Mary Janes in a C width. Not as sexy as my old shoes, but pretty and femme enough for dressing up.

Halloween 1998, I was in New York for the weekend. Saturday night I had supper with friends in Chelsea and then got in a cab to go back to my hotel in SoHo. When the cab got stuck in a traffic jam caused by the Halloween parade, the cabdriver told me to get out and walk. Downtown Manhattan was filled with wildly dressed people celebrating; I was definitely not part of that. I was wearing my suede dress shoes; by the time I got to SoHo, my feet were killing me. Back in my hotel, I discovered nearly a dozen blisters.

March 2001, Dick and I had taken our oldest, Max, to New York for his fifteenth birthday. We were walking all over Manhattan, showing him the sights. I was wearing my forest-green Chuck Taylors. The second day, my left foot started to hurt, so badly that I couldn't really walk much. New York City and walking: it's a long story for me.

· · ·

Back in Milwaukee, the pain did not go away, and a couple months later, I went to an orthopedic surgeon who specialized in feet. After X-rays, he came in to tell me what he saw, what was going on with my feet. He talked for maybe a half hour. I don't have a clear sense of what he said, and yet many of his phrases are burned in my memory: that I had inverted arches and my ligaments were shot (I had been born with flat feet and apparently my arches had "fallen"); that there were twenty-seven bones in the foot and that the ligaments held them in place, but that mine no longer did; that the problem was three-dimensional, and I needed lace-up shoes to hold the bones in position; that I needed to wear orthotics and special orthopedic shoes. I remember his mocking the green Chuck Taylors I'd come in wearing, folding and squeezing them to show just how inadequate they were for the task. I remember his expressed contempt for the shoes women wear. I remember his saying that, unless I heeded his advice, in ten years I would not be able to walk, not be able to stand on my feet.

By the time I left his office, I was pretty much in shock. I felt light-headed and confused; I'm not sure how I managed to drive home. I remember feeling very alone, not quite in my body, and definitely not in my familiar life. I had walked into that doctor's office thinking I had some minor, transitory problem and that there would be some therapeutic solution, thinking there was a small problem with a small, remote part of my body; I walked out stricken with a sense of catastrophic loss. I felt he had handed down a life sentence: ugly shoes without parole.

I remained more or less in that state for a few months, depressed and anxious. My concern was not my feet, nor my ability to walk; I could not accept the loss of my shoes. I was condemned to wear clodhoppers, shoes that would not go with any clothes. There was no way to look good in such shoes; I would look ugly, ridiculous, unfeminine.

I dutifully went to the orthopedic shoe store and bought several pairs of the least ugly of the shoes, trying to salvage some remnant of style. The problem was not just the shoes, but what to wear with them. It was summer: dresses, skirts, shorts, and lightweight, flow-ing pants all looked hideous with these heavy shoes. I wore jeans all summer, despite the heat—that was the least bad look. I remember thinking that I wished I were butch, that my shoes forced me to dress more butch.

I wore the shoes, tried to look presentable, longed for sandals. My pain did not go away or even lessen, and I was depressed. One day, a couple months after my diagnosis, in a desperate burst of energy, I threw fifty pairs of shoes from my closet into garbage bags and carried them out to the trash cans in the alley. I couldn't even bear to donate them to a place like Goodwill, because I had to get them out of my house right away. Fifty, I counted them: all my beautiful shoes, which I so loved. Actually, not all; I kept a half dozen of my very favorite pairs, displayed on a shelf, although I would never wear them again.

. . .

It took several years to resign myself to the loss of my beautiful shoes. During that time, I underwent a battery of medical treatments: prescription anti-inflammatories, physical therapy, ankle brace, cortisone injection, walking boot, and even surgery. I changed foot doctors, found a podiatrist with an Italian surname who wore beautiful leather shoes and seemed to understand why women would want to wear the sorts of shoes I loved. I asked if I could ever wear heels, and he replied that I could if, say, I were just going out to dinner, not going to be much on my feet. Over a year after my surgery, on my birthday, I put on a dress and the only pair of heels I had that could contain my substantial orthotics, and went off to a fashionable restaurant to celebrate. It felt great to be wearing a dress, but after dinner I could not walk the few steps from the table back to the car that a valet had brought to the front door.

Although the surgery did get rid of the original pain (tendonitis in the left instep), after the year it took to recover, I learned that the reprieve from pain was only temporary, that I could not go back to wearing cute shoes, that I would never wear heels or sandals again. That, however sympathetic a doctor I might find, there was to be no reprieve from ugly shoes, not even for a special occasion.

Forced to accept my clodhopper fate, I began finally to focus on what was going on with my feet. My ligaments were too stretched out to hold my bones in position. Sturdy tie shoes and aggressive orthotics could do that, but only for a while. When I was on my feet for more than a few minutes, the weight of my body pushed my foot bones out of position and into pain. While ugly shoes bought me the ability to be on my feet, they could not restore me to full mobility. Even in the most supportive shoes, I could not spend more than thirty minutes on my feet (walking or standing) because the pain became worse and worse until I sat down. As I learned to manage these limitations, I stopped mourning my beautiful shoes.

A few years after my surgery, Dick and I went to New York for a little vacation. The first day we were there, I was so excited to be in the city, I decided to walk the twenty blocks from our hotel to the restaurant where we had a reservation. Wearing ample orthotics and sturdy walking shoes, I thought twenty blocks was not really that much, and I so wanted to walk the streets, which had always been my favorite thing about being in New York. As I walked, I felt energized and happy, reconnected to decades of pleasurable walking in Manhattan. By the time we got to the restaurant, my feet were so sore I could not stand. The next two days we took cabs whenever we went out, and I fell into a depression. This was not being in New York. Usually a trip to New York meant great sex in the hotel room, away from the kids and turned on by the city. This time, in the hotel, rather than getting turned on, I cried. I felt a profound sense of loss, no longer for my shoes, but for some sexiness the city made me feel.

We stopped going to New York for pleasure trips, but a few years later Dick and I and our youngest, Ruby, are in the city for a family event. By this time (2008), we have learned to take a wheelchair along when we travel so we can walk the city streets and see the sites. Sunday we have brunch with friends in Tribeca, and afterward we walk to SoHo so twelve-year-old Ruby can shop. Sunday afternoon, SoHo is full of shoppers; rolling along crowded sidewalks in a wheelchair, not being at eye level, is a new experience for me. Everyone seems attractive, energetic, stylish, and, though I am literally surrounded by people, I feel isolated on a different level. It is not an unpleasant experience.

Some months later, while having sex at home in my own bed, I am surprised to find myself in my head back in the wheelchair on the sidewalks of SoHo, surrounded by attractive young people, all oblivious to my presence. It is as if the wheelchair makes me invisible. Sitting in the wheelchair, with people all around me, I unzip my pants and pull my cock out. Exposing myself in a crowd makes me hard, and I start jerking off. No one notices. In this dense crowd, my head surrounded by bodies—breasts and bellies and buttocks—bodies close enough to touch but unaware of me, my huge cock spurts a sticky, white mess. As my wheelchaired cock ejaculates in my mental SoHo, in my Milwaukee bed my body spasms a great big come.

. . .

The Ending

I had to tell this story. For several years, the story kept composing itself in my head: details would accumulate, phrases and narrative sequences. And while this obsessive thinking never went beyond working on the narrative, I always imagined that, once written, the story would become an occasion for crip theory, theorizing at the intersection of sexuality and disability. In fact, my motivation for telling the story was a sense of what it had to offer for such theorizing. During the years of this obsessive composing, I was reading around in crip theory, and whenever I read a particularly compelling essay, I would soon find myself working on this story in my head.

After writing the story, I showed it to a few friends. Each of these readers remarked at what a shock the last paragraph is. The story ends with a twist; this is not where the narrative seems to be heading. The ending is not just a surprise for the reader; when that wheelchair fantasy popped into my head, it came as a complete surprise to me. It was the power of this surprise, as I experienced it, that made me want to tell the story. I felt I had to communicate this surprise, to communicate my sudden revelation that disability and sexuality did not have to have the relationship that felt inevitable.

This idea of surprise is crucial to what I want to talk about here. I want to think about the relation between the ending fantasy and the narrative arc that precedes it. Such a surprise ending is not unusual in narrative; it is, for example, arguably the staple of a certain kind of short story. But I am interested in thinking about this relation between ending and narrative unfolding not in fiction, but in how we understand our lives as we live them in time. The surprise I am interested in is not the reader's surprise, but my amazement when this fantasy appeared for the first time in my head. I wrote the story in order to transmit and contemplate that lived surprise.

The surprise here has to do with what I need to call the phallus; this is a story about a phallic surprise. Up until the final paragraph, this seems to be a story about castration. The loss of sexy shoes, and then the loss of the ability to walk the streets, could be understood as castration narrative: I "had it," sexiness, uprightness, and then I "lost it," once and for all. But then the phallus reappears, surprisingly, miraculously, in the ending. The phallus, for my purposes here, is definitely that huge bursting cock in my head as the story ends, but it is also those high heels in the earlier parts of the story. And it is New York City, too (the Big Apple as phallus). In the standard narrative we call castration anxiety, once the phallus is lost, it is lost forever. I hear that "forever," for example, when the story's second section ends with "I would never wear them again." While my story is thoroughly riddled with castration, this is a story of how the lost phallus is found again—and in the place where we least expect it, a place marked by the narrative arc as the very seat of castration.

I have imagined that this story would allow us to rethink the relation between the phallus and disability. Finding the phallus in the wheelchair in my head not only reverses the direction of my personal narrative; it runs counter to widespread cultural constructions of the wheelchair as site of castration. The locus classicus of this is undoubtedly D. H. Lawrence's *Lady Chatterley's Lover*, where

Lord Chatterley in his wheelchair is the castrated foil to the phallic hero, Mellors. If the phallus can appear in a wheelchair, and not just coincidentally but *if the wheelchair is conjured in order to make the phallus appear*, then the relation between phallus and wheelchair, the symbolic relation between sexuality and disability, is not what we might think.

It has been my hope that this story will allow us to rethink the place of the phallus, to recognize how various are the places it can appear. As I conceived and framed this account, place was central: I organized it around a series of incidents that all occurred in the same locale, New York City. The sidewalk and the wheelchair are also significant places in the story. But it is not only the places of the phallus that this story engages. The sequential relation between phallic ending and prior castration narrative has led me to realize that this is also very much a story about the temporalities of the phallus. And this awareness of a temporal dimension has occasioned an important expansion in my theoretical framework.

Interested in adding temporality to my analysis, I began to supplement my reading in crip theory with texts from aging studies. And so it was that, soon after I had composed the above account, I read Margaret Morganroth Gullette's *Declining to Decline*, a book that theorizes aging in "the midlife." *Declining* begins with a few autobiographical anecdotes in order to introduce its central concept, the decline story. One of Gullette's anecdotes strikes me as uncannily familiar. At the age of forty-nine, suffering from acute back pain, Gullette goes to see an orthopedic surgeon and leaves in a state of abject loss. "I had just gotten the worst news of my personal life. . . . I was plunged into planning my suicide," she writes.[1] Like Gullette, I consulted an orthopedic surgeon at the age of forty-nine. Although it is her back that aches whereas my pain was in my left foot, I am struck by the similarities between Gullette's response to the orthopedic surgeon and mine: as I put it in my narrative, "I walked out stricken with a sense of catastrophic loss. I felt he had handed down a life sentence."

Declining to Decline explains that such moments of entrance into catastrophic loss typify our culture's construction of middle age.

Reading Gullette, I realized that the story I tell here, which I had thought of as a story about disability, is also in fact a story about aging. Gullette's work on and resistance to the decline story has become an important theoretical companion for this chapter. Connecting my story here to Gullette's story, seeing the importance of the temporal dimension in what I wanted to tell, expanded my theoretical framework from two terms to three: to the nexus of sexuality and disability, I now would add aging.

Gullette concludes the chapter on her midlife back pain thus: "Chronic suffering takes different forms: if we ever begin to listen, the sufferers will have a lot of alternative stories to tell. Inexorability doesn't express the way our waves of knowledge come to us, the way we discover our private response at the same time we endure what feels like bodily injustice."[2] I would like to think of the story I am telling here as one of the "alternative stories" Gullette asks us to listen to, stories that can provide alternatives to what she here calls inexorability. Inexorability is another name for the decline story; it is the temporal logic of our culture's construction of aging. I recognize it as another name for the standard temporality of castration.

It is, to be sure, the final paragraph of my story that most powerfully counters inexorability. The ending is the most important piece of what I want to explore about temporality and the phallus, the most stunning evidence for rethinking sexuality and disability; it is the ending that made me want to tell this story. Yet the ending's power depends on the fact that what leads up to it is a pretty standard decline story. It is precisely because the story to that point is such a recognizable castration narrative that the last paragraph seems to promise an alteration in our understanding of phallic temporalities.

The alternative temporality I am interested in is not just the happy ending but the coexistence of that happy surprise with the decline story. Since the ending is, for a variety of reasons, foremost in our heads when we finish reading the narrative, it seemed necessary to begin here by talking about the ending. But I also worry that the story's last paragraph threatens to erase what comes before. In order to do justice to what precedes the ending, I will defer my discussion of the phallus in the wheelchair until later. Before that, I will look at a few other topics engaged by this narrative: city sidewalks, feminism and high heels, and gender and disability.

City Sidewalks

When I first drafted the story that opens this chapter, I gave it the title "City Sidewalks." The narrative contains a series of events, spanning forty years, which took place on New York sidewalks, events connected by their location. In 2010 Eliza Chandler proposed in an article in *Disability Studies Quarterly* a genre she calls "sidewalk stories."

In the introduction to her article Chandler writes: "This paper explores the troubling task of identifying as, with and for disability through sidewalks and the stories they provoke."[3] Chandler's focus in this article is on disability identity, and her most valuable theoretical contribution is her insistence that we learn to think through the entanglement of disability pride with disability shame, but along the way to making this argument she casually suggests that there is something called sidewalk stories.

Chandler uses the phrase repeatedly and evocatively without ever quite explaining what such a genre is. Aside from serving as the title, the phrase appears three times in Chandler's essay. The first time, about halfway through, she writes: "I have many stories of disability, sidewalk stories and others, tucked into my body that collectively bring sense to my 'being-in-the-world' as disabled." Sidewalk stories, it seems, are a subset, a subgenre, of "stories of disability." While "tucked into my body" suggests something quite private and interior, "being-in-the-world" implies the public and exterior. Chandler's sidewalks might be a zone of encounter between private body and public world.

Chandler's title phrase appears twice in the concluding section of the essay: "I return now to where I began, in sidewalk stories, to discover what new stories . . . the togetherness of pride and shame might release into the world. . . . I tell these sidewalk stories . . . because when they are not released into the world they dwell in my body, festering in shame. In my stories and their telling, pride and shame materialize together." As in the earlier instance, sidewalk stories engage the opposition between "dwelling in my body" and "release into the world," the opposition between private and public. Here in the conclusion, that opposition also involves the affective polarity pride and shame.

While Chandler never really defines what she means by sidewalk stories, she tells one at the beginning of her essay. The story involves walking, disability, and an encounter with strangers. It is, as she puts it in her conclusion, a story of "the unbearable shame of being laughed at on a street corner on a nighttime walk." While it is a story of shame, her essay's conclusion suggests that telling the story manifests not just shame but also pride: "I tell these stories because when they are not released into the world they dwell in my body, festering in shame. In my stories and in their telling . . . pride rubs shame, pride comforts shame." While the story is about "unbearable shame," while the story untold "festers in shame," telling the story joins pride to shame. That is why Chandler tells sidewalk stories.

I like Chandler's insistence on the entanglement of pride and shame. Although "Sidewalk Stories" does not talk about sexuality, her insistence on entangling pride with shame resonates with a similar move in queer theory. In the introduction to the 2009 book *Gay Shame*, the volume's editors write: "Gay pride has never been able to separate itself entirely from shame, or to transcend shame. Gay pride does not even make sense without some reference to the shame of being gay, and its very successes (to say nothing of its failures) testify to the intensity of its ongoing struggle with shame."[4] Although the topic here is *gay* pride and shame, the assertion of the entanglement of pride and shame is remarkably consistent with Chandler's.

Gay Shame in fact includes a section titled "Disabled Shame." Reading the essays in that section of the anthology a few years ago was one of the strongest triggers to composing my foot memoir in my head. My sidewalk story insisted on being told in this particular framework, where disabled shame is part of a more general queer inquiry into the relation of shame and pride.

While Chandler's sidewalk story is not about sexuality, two years later Riva Lehrer published one very much about sexuality, "Golem Girl Gets Lucky." Like Chandler, Lehrer combines telling stories from her life with theorizing disability. Chandler and Lehrer not only tell sidewalk stories; both do anecdotal theory. In her "Golem Girl," Lehrer provides us with a candid, gutsy theorization of the sexuality of the sidewalk.

"All women know that the sidewalk is a catwalk," Lehrer writes.[5] A catwalk is "a narrow ramp extending from the stage into the audience in a theatre, nightclub, etc, [especially] as used by models in a fashion show."[6] Lehrer imagines the sidewalk as some sort of beauty pageant: "We are judged on the quality of our flesh. And my entry in the pageant is a body that's more Z-shaped than S-curved."[7] While "catwalk" gestures toward the "pageant," I suspect it also carries allusions to what a paragraph later she calls "the pussy dance," referring still to the pageant of female flesh. Lehrer's "catwalk" might have shades of the "cathouse," too.

Like Chandler, Lehrer looks at the sidewalk as a site of disability "in-the-world." Lehrer fills in some of the history behind disability on the sidewalk: "Even though we've always been here, we lived in back rooms . . . and nursing homes, trapped by stairs and manual chairs and sheer bloody prejudice. We began to appear along with curb cuts, electric doors, and kneeling buses."[8] Where once disabled bodies were "trapped," hidden away, they have "beg[un] to appear," to move from private, interior space out to the sidewalk. The dynamic Chandler emphasizes for sidewalk stories, a movement from private interior to public exterior, is what happens on Lehrer's sidewalk. Chandler connects this to shame and pride, to the encounter between "body" and "world"; Lehrer makes explicit that such encounters are sexual. Not only does she call the sidewalk a catwalk, but she refers to "the sidewalk mating dance": "In the sidewalk mating dance we're winnowed out as undesirable." Lehrer is eloquent about how her body is undesirable: "My entry in the pageant is a body that's more Z-shaped than S-curved. . . . She should sway with a spine strung in a sinuous rosary of bones. . . . She should undulate with a hide-and-seek of the hips and the breasts."[9] The catwalk is not just a place to be seen and judged; the catwalk is a place where a woman walks. If the sidewalk is a catwalk, it is because both are places for walking.

And the desirability of bodies thereon depends on how bodies move when walking: "She should sway. . . . She should undulate. . . . Sometimes we . . . call her a Streetwalker." Sway, undulate, these are ways that women walk (ways of walking that are heightened by high heels). That this paragraph ends on the word "Streetwalker" amplifies these connections between walking and sexuality: sidewalk, catwalk, streetwalker. "She should undulate with a hide-and-seek of the hips and breasts. . . . Sometimes we punish her for the power of her gravitational field and call her a Streetwalker. Some women opt out of the pussy dance and choose kinetic defenses."[10] Lehrer's view of the normative feminine walk is not just envious; it includes her awareness of the dangers of being seen as desirable female flesh on the sidewalk.

Lehrer also includes an awareness that disabled entries into the pageant are not simply undesirable. "I will be one of the crip girls whose bodies scare the panel of judges," she writes. "They are afraid that our unbalanced shapes hint of unsanctioned desires. On both sides of the bed."[11] The judges are scared because they can indeed imagine desire for the disabled body. It is not that the crip girl body is simply undesirable; it is that the desire she elicits is "unsanctioned."

Chandler's sidewalk stories are ambivalent sites of "the togetherness of pride and shame." Lehrer's explicitly sexualized sidewalks are sites where approval of normative femininity can slide into shaming attack, where undesirable might also mean unsanctioned desire. Lehrer's tone ranges from the sadly ignored ("they don't look long enough to decide whether we're attractive") to the defiantly queer ("I will be one of the crip girls whose bodies scare").[12] As Chandler puts it, "Here pride rubs shame, pride comforts shame."

Lehrer's "I will be one of the crip girls . . ." is what Chandler calls "identifying as disabled with pride." I understand Lehrer's sexualized account of the sidewalk in conjunction with Chandler's disabled pride and shame. I connect Chandler's pride to Lehrer's defiant embrace of her body as emblem of unsanctioned sexuality. I connect Chandler's shame to Lehrer's account of her body as undesirable. Looking at an explicitly sexualized pride and shame, I find myself wondering about the relation between pride and the phallus, between shame and castration.

Lehrer's theorization of sidewalks helps make sense of my story. In my wheelchair in SoHo surrounded by bodies, I felt invisible. Lehrer writes: "Canes and chairs . . . disrupt the pedestrian flow. The crowd streams around us like rocks in the river, staring at and ignoring us in strange proportions. . . . They don't look long enough to decide whether we're attractive or not."[13] Yet later, on the sidewalk in my head, those very "crowds stream[ing] around us" enabled my sexuality; their not looking long enough provided me with unsanctioned opportunity.

Lehrer is particularly acute at explaining the erotic sidewalk in the head: "We navigate a daily pageant of human variation. . . . All those different bodies offer a catalogue that lets us discover the shape of our lusts. Our libidos become engorged on memories of bodies we've briefly seen."[14] Back home, I discovered a new shape to my lust; my libido became engorged on my memory of being in a stream of bodies on the sidewalk. "Our libidos become engorged"—here's the phallus; "on memories of bodies we've briefly seen"—here's the phallus at the end of my narrative.

The pageant in this paragraph of Lehrer's seems different from the one in the catwalk-to-Streetwalker paragraph; this vision of sidewalk sexuality here is broader. Rather than the normative "She *should* sway. . . . She *should* undulate," we have "human variation" and "all those different bodies." Rather than women being "judged," rather than "the panel of judges," there is a general "we" who on the sidewalk "discover the shape of our lusts," whose "libidos become engorged on memories of bodies we've briefly seen."

The sidewalk pageant can be a "catalogue," a site where we shop for what we want. Lehrer uses the image of a catalogue to discuss the dynamics of our desire for bodies encountered on the sidewalk. My story connects that desire with the less explicitly sexual desire aroused by shopping. I am interested in that as an aspect of sexuality: the props we desire and the fantasies of how those props make us desirable. Lehrer's sidewalk is a catalogue of the bodies that engorge our desire, the bodies we desire to have; my sidewalks offer that, but they also offer a catalogue of the bodies we desire to be. In addition to Lehrer's pageant of different bodies, the sidewalk in my account is also the site of window-shopping.

When I gave my little story the title "City Sidewalks," the phrase came to me from a song long-inscribed in my memory. The Christmas song "Silver Bells" opens: "City sidewalks, busy sidewalks." This is a song about shopping during the holiday season, "as the shoppers rush home with their treasures."[15] It seems strange, even to me, to connect my narrative to a Christmas song.

My relation to Christmas songs has always been ambivalent. As a Jewish girl, I never celebrated Christmas, but I felt both excited and excluded not by the actual holiday but by the experience of shopping during the month before Christmas, surrounded by carols and holiday decorations: as the song puts it, "In the air there's a feeling of Christmas." I felt excited and excluded by the anticipation of the big event I would never celebrate. My relation to Christmas seems a lot like my relation to New York City. I never lived there, but I regularly found myself excited to be on those busy sidewalks, surrounded by others, feeling the anticipation and desire for what seemed to be "in the air."

The allusion to "Silver Bells" that occurred to me as a title for my memoir has to do with sidewalks as places of shopping. Not so much with buying goods, but precisely shopping, with the anticipation and desire for getting the "treasure," the Big Apple, the fullness of some later consummation that for me is the excitement and sexiness of city sidewalks. For me, city sidewalks are indeed, as Lehrer puts it, a "catalogue."

The window-shopping in my story displays a marked preference for a particular type of window: "windows full of women's shoes." I am far from alone in this particular orientation. An article in a consumer research journal concludes: "Shoes are a key target for consumer fantasies and indulgence. It is little wonder that shoe stores dominate the shopping mall. . . . Shoes are an important object of desire and delight. . . . Even when they are flippant and frivolous, shoes are serious objects of hope, joy, and sorrow."[16] A woman interviewed for the book *Shoes: A Lexicon of Style* said that buying shoes constitutes "the highest form of shopping."[17]

As I put it in my "City Sidewalks" confession, "During the 1970s . . . I remember walking and walking in the city, turned on by the lure of window-shopping. The windows that spoke to me were filled with gorgeous shoes, high-heeled numbers in a lush array of colors and shapes. Whatever I wanted from New York, whatever New York made me want, was embodied in those windows full of women's shoes."

Feminism and High Heels

In the 1970s, while I was lusting after them in New York windows, "high heels were viewed very unsympathetically by feminists."[18] I was a '70s feminist. I remember other feminists asking how I could be a feminist and wear those shoes. The feminist disapproval heightened my desire for high heels: they were unsanctioned.

In an article published in 2001, Lorraine Gamman gives a brief history of the late twentieth-century feminist take on high heels. This history begins with the 1970s critique, and then "the feminist rejection . . . started to lose much of its grassroots support in the postmodern context of the 1980s. The idea that . . . sexy shoes were not simply oppressive, but offered pleasure to women, became more widely accepted. . . . High heels . . . clearly connote feminine sexiness, and [in the 1990s] at a moment when some feminists decided to reclaim female desire and lead a rebellion against neutered sexuality . . . high heels were *almost* seen as *politically correct* attire for desiring subjects."[19]

In this account, between the 1970s and the 1990s high heels do something like a 180-degree pivot in their relation to feminism, going from politically incorrect to "almost" the opposite. While much has been written about the relation between '70s feminism and '90s feminism,[20] I want here to focus on the ambiguous status of high heels, on how they could possibly symbolize both female oppression and female power.

I take Gamman as a companion in this inquiry—for reasons that are in part anecdotal. During her study of shoes, Gamman makes a small personal disclosure: "Despite the success of high heels in the 1990s . . . some 'strong' women were left behind wearing sneakers. . . . It took me a long time before I let myself realize that the expensive heeled objects of my desire would never be more than a one-night stand."[21] Note here the 1990s expectation that "'strong' women" would wear high heels. While that will be important for my consideration of the ambivalent relation between heels and female power, I actually quote this passage because of Gamman's remark that rather than wearing heels, she was wearing sneakers.[22] By the 1990s I was wearing Converse high-tops. I appreciate how Gamman's language reflects her erotic relation to high heels ("heeled objects of my desire," "one-night stand"), but I am even more moved by the recognition that I was not the only one who felt "left behind wearing sneakers" in the 1990s. It is not just sneakers that Gamman and I share, but the sadness and sense of loss ("left behind"), the loss of something sexual.

Looking at "the success of high heels in the 1990s," Gamman cites two different meanings they carry. First (quoting Tom Ford of Gucci): "It's hard not to be sexy in a pair of high heels." On the other hand (quoting Simon Doonan of Barney's, New York): "High heels create a level of authority."[23] The very same double meaning shows up in other feminist discussions of high heels. For example, Claudia Wobovnik in 2013 states, "On the one hand, women in high heels are perceived as glamorous, sexy and seductive, and on the other, women in important positions wear high heels to communicate authority and power."[24] Wobovnik considers the coexistence of these two meanings "paradoxical." Symbolizing both sex and authority is paradoxical according to our usual assumptions that those two are not only different but actually at odds. The fact that high heels carry both meanings suggests they operate in a register where these meanings are entangled rather than opposed.

It is right after quoting Ford and Doonan on the two meanings of high heels that Gamman makes her sad confession that "some 'strong' women were left behind wearing sneakers." While I first noted (for anecdotal reasons) the sneakers in this sentence, I would now like to think about the "'strong' women," about the strong-in-quotation-marks here. The phrase "strong women" also appears two pages earlier in this history of feminism's relation to high heels: "The feminist rejection . . . started to lose much of its grassroots support in . . . the 1980s. . . . It was hard to make the case stick that women's fashion shoes were linked to female subordination when so many strong (so-called phallic women) wore them."[25]

In this earlier passage, while "strong" is not in quotation marks, there is a parenthesis to explain what the adjective means, and the word introduced to explain "strong" has somewhat questionable status as "so-called."[26] Protected by this double hedge of parenthesis and so-called, Gamman introduces into her account of feminism the idea of phallic women. This hedged appearance of "phallic women" suggests that, while the phrase may not be one Gamman can endorse, it is nonetheless useful to explain why high heels were able to change valence for feminists.

I can certainly imagine why Gamman might feel the need to hedge, might be uncomfortable using "phallic" in this context. The later part of her article moves away from feminist cultural history into a more psychoanalytic frame for considering the meaning of high heels. The significance of "phallic" in that later section is quite different than in the early parenthesis. For example: "As a cultural sign, the reading of the female shoe has been dominated by the idea that the heel is a penis substitute and symbolizes phallic replacement."[27] Wanting to resist the dominant reading of female shoes, wanting a female-affirmative understanding of the place of shoes in women's sexuality, Gamman opposes the traditional psychoanalytic model, a model in which women are lacking, needing "penis substitutes" and "phallic replacement." In the dominant psychoanalytic model, the phallus underwrites female inadequacy. A feminist cannot help but be uncomfortable with the concept of the phallus given its function in the normative psychoanalytic understanding of women as castrated.

Despite this serious drawback, Gamman nonetheless uses "phallic" (albeit in parenthesis and only "so-called") to characterize strong, feminist women affirming our sexuality. If I linger here on Gamman's parenthetic, unsanctioned phallus, it is because in it I catch a fleeting glimpse of a phallus such as I am proposing here in this book—not the normative psychoanalytic phallus, but an alternative phallus, a phallus that might be claimed by a feminist.

For my purposes in this chapter, I note that this phallus, a woman's phallus, is associated with wearing heels. Immediately after citing the two meanings of high heels, Gamman refers to "'strong' women," a phrase echoing her affirmative, if unsanctioned, use of "phallic women." If Gamman, despite her misgivings, uses "phallic," is it because that term can bring together the two seemingly disparate meanings of high heels? Because sexy and authority can meet in the paradoxical concept of the phallic woman?

"No other item of attire has such a positive phallic identity as the high heel," states William A. Rossi in his book *The Sex Life of the Foot and the Shoe*.[28] Although Rossi's book is, to be sure, dated and hardly feminist, I value its enthusiasm for high heels and especially the way its enthusiasm leads to a delineation of what it calls "a positive phallic identity." The dominant reading of the high heel as phallic replacement cited by Gamman is what I would call a negative phallic identity, where the woman's shoe as a substitute marks her lack of a penis. Gamman's "phallic women," on the other hand, far from lacking, could be an example of positive phallic identity.

Like Gamman, Rossi seems to be a real fan of high heels. In Rossi's book, high heels have a strikingly phallic effect, both on wearers and on admirers. Rossi quotes one Dr. Ullerstam: "When women's fashion decrees high-heeled boots, many men walk the streets with a perpetual erection."[29] "Many men," "perpetual erection": this is definitely hyperbole. Rossi's enthusiastic hyperbole is not just restricted to the effect of heels on men: "Not diamonds but high heels have always been a girl's best friend. They've done more for psy-chosexual uplift than any other article of fashion or clothing ever devised."[30] While less literal than Ullerstam's "perpetual erection," the "psychosexual uplift" here still sounds phallic to me. "More . . . than any other article of . . . clothing ever devised" recalls Rossi's earlier "no other item of attire has such a positive phallic identity." In Rossi's enthusiasm, the high heel is always "the most"; we might call this hyperbolic inflation phallic rhetoric.

Like Gamman, I am all too aware of the way the traditional psy-choanalytic notion of the phallus has reinforced ideas of female sex-ual inadequacy, so-called castration. I am interested in a different no-tion of the phallus, one I might call, following Rossi, a positive phallic identity. I associate that positive phallic identity with Gamman's women in heels, paradoxically conveying both sex and authority.

Yet what makes Gamman's "strong" women in heels most per-suasively phallic for me is that she contemplates them from the poi-gnant viewpoint of "left behind wearing sneakers," a perspective I might call high-heel envy. In calling it that, I speak from experi-ence: I believe that women in heels are phallic because, in my life story, the loss of high heels feels like castration.

· · ·

Gamman, Rossi, and Wobovnik have helped me conceptualize how high heels are phallic. I turned to them because the notion that heels can make one feel phallic is crucial to understanding my story, understanding how losing the ability to wear heels made me feel castrated. Gamman and Wobovnik are feminist thinkers; Rossi and Gamman use psychoanalytic theory. Not one of these theorists of high heels has a crip perspective; and yet there is a moment in all three of their discussions of heels when the issue of disability arises. This suggests to me that there could be a crip perspective on high heels.

For Wobovnik, disability is a final aspect of the "paradoxical" that generally characterizes women's relation to high heels: "Cer-tain readings of high-heeled shoes are quite paradoxical. Yet an-other absurd example entails the question of pain and medical impairment. . . . Rather than abandoning high heels because of health risks, women bear discomfort, pain, and physical impairments to reap the symbolic benefits of high-heeled shoes."[31]

While Wobovnik is troubled by women's paradoxical relation to heels, Rossi, in his enthusiasm for their sexiness, heartily embraces the paradox: "The American Medical Association, the American Podiatry Association, the National Safety Council, and various other authoritative bodies have issued public warnings about the danger of wearing . . . high heels. . . . As usual, these well-intentioned spokesmen are out of tune with the realities of female psychology. Just as a courageous soldier is willing to risk his life in war, so a woman is willing to risk hers in the perennial battle for sex attraction, and all the dangers and warnings be damned."[32] Rossi makes a hero out of the woman in heels, courageously flouting the advice of medical authorities.

The risk of disability also appears in Gamman's account of the 1970s feminist take on heels: "High heels were viewed very unsympathetically by feminists, many of whom saw them as . . . literally involved in crippling women." Feminists of the 1970s did not just see high heels as collaborating with female subordination; they saw a connection between high heels and wheelchairs.

I was a '70s feminist. I scoffed at their sense that high heels signified female subordination. I welcomed the '90s feminist embrace of heels, although by then I was no longer able to wear them. The feminist connection between high heels and wheelchairs is not so easy for me to scoff at. In my story, I descend from high heels not just to sneakers but finally into a wheelchair, a descent from positive phallic identity to something like castration. I never consider the possibility (the likelihood?) that my beloved heels actually caused my foot troubles.[33]

There is one additional allusion to disability in Gamman's history of feminism and high heels. To exemplify the feminist rejection of heels, Gamman quotes Susan Brownmiller in her book *Femininity*: "A feminine shoe imposes a new problem of grace and self consciousness on what otherwise would be a simple act of locomotion, and in this artful handicap lies its subjugation and supposed charm."[34] This is different from Gamman's earlier phrase "crippling women," which suggests, as does Wobovnik, that wearing heels causes "physical impairments." Brownmiller's "artful handicap" implies that wearing heels simulates a handicap, making the woman who could otherwise simply walk appear as if she had mobility issues.

I am drawn to this idea of the artful handicap, perhaps perversely. Although "artful" here means artificial, not genuine, it also suggests aesthetic achievement, beauty. Brownmiller's artful handicap not only connects disability and "subjugation," but also disability and "supposed charm." She imagines someone (not her) who finds this handicap charming, that is, attractive, sexy. I try to imagine a crip reading of Brownmiller's phrase.

In my story, disability keeps me from wearing heels, and not being able to wear heels feels like a handicap ("left behind wearing sneakers," as Gamman puts it). Not being able to wear heels because of my disability keeps me from looking sexy. In Brownmiller's view, on the other hand, wearing heels produces a handicapped walk that is itself sexy. For Brownmiller, artful handicap is clearly a bad thing, but as someone who not only loves feminine shoes but is far removed from walking as "a simple act of locomotion," I find myself wanting to wring a crip twist on the artful handicap, imagining how this phrase could bring together my high heels and my wheelchair in art and charm and sexiness.

Gender and Disability

By opposing walking in feminine shoes to "what otherwise would be a simple act of locomotion," Susan Brownmiller invokes an image of normative mobility and contrasts it with gendered walking. In Brownmiller's radical feminist perspective, normal mobility is not gendered and feminine walking is a "handicap." Reading in crip theory provides a quite different perspective, where normative walking is gendered, and disability produces gender trouble.

Eli Clare's *Exile and Pride*, one of the first books to combine queer and disability perspectives, is now a classic text of crip theory. Clare is particularly articulate on the subject of gender and walking: "The mannerisms that help define gender—the ways in which people walk, swing their hips . . . take up space with their bodies— are all based upon how nondisabled people move. A woman who walks with crutches does not walk like a 'woman'; a man who uses a wheelchair . . . does not move like a 'man.' The construction of gender depends not only upon the male body and female body, but also upon the nondisabled body."[35]

Reading Clare's "the ways in which people walk, swing their hips," we might think of Riva Lehrer's "She should sway. . . . She should undulate." In her sense of the disabled body's exclusion from gender norms, Lehrer explicitly references how this is at odds with a certain feminist idea: "Women's studies has taught us to see the damage caused by rigid gendering. But there is a different kind of confusion and hurt caused by its absence, when it's clear that you're not being included because you've been disqualified. Disabled women must continually claim their gender in the face of active erasure."[36]

In their writings, Clare and Lehrer give enough of their personal stories that we know both are lifelong nonnormative walkers. Their experience as thus excluded from gender norms results in a particularly valuable reconsideration of gender, especially since both are well versed in feminist theory. Both recognize the importance of the feminist critique of rigid gendering but insist on amplifying and altering that from the perspective of disabled gender trouble. As valuable as Clare and Lehrer are for explicating the relation between gender and normative walking, the temporality of their disability is not mine. For understanding my story, I am drawn to a group of writers whose crip gender trouble comes upon them in adult life, wreaking havoc upon their already-formed gender identities.

I will here cite three of these writers. Not only because they display the same disability temporality as my narrative but also because the gender identities threatened by their disabilities are not male-female but, like mine, butch-femme. (I wrote: "I remember thinking that I wished I were butch, that my shoes forced me to dress more butch.")

In a collection of butch-femme writings published in 1992, I found Mary Frances Platt writing about wheelchair use and femme identity: "As lives go, mine changed: slowly at first and then more dramatically. Recurring back pain and limited range of motion. . . . Soon after came decreased mobility. . . . I . . . began to use a three-wheeled power chair. The more disabled I became, the more I mourned the ways my sexual femme self had manifested through the nondisabled me."[37]

The temporality of her story recalls mine; her life "changed," a slow decline ending in a wheelchair. Platt titles her essay "Reclaiming Femme . . . Again" because she frames her difficulty claiming femme identity after disability as a repetition of an earlier difficulty: "The seventies brand of white feminism had me trimming my nails and cutting off my hair. Soon I was outfitted in farmer jeans and high tops. . . . Eventually, I pulled the pieces of my being back together and proclaimed boldly, 'I am a working-class lesbian femme.' So, I had maybe six years of . . . unleashing my seductive femme self when, as lives go, mine changed."[38] Fighting against the loss of femme identity because of her disability feels like a repetition of her fight against the 1970s feminist rejection of that identity.

I identify with Platt's relation to '70s feminism (not to mention those high-tops), and even more with her mourning her "femme self," but what I love most about her essay is a sexy twist she gives to the image of the wheelchair: "I hang out more with the sexual outlaws now—you know, the motorcycle lesbians who see wheels and chrome between your legs as something exciting."[39]

An essay published a few years later in a collection of lesbian writing on disability tells a similar story of femme identity threatened by disability. Like Platt, Sharon Wachsler has chronic fatigue immune dysfunction syndrome, but Wachsler also has multiple chemical sensitivity. Although she feels a similar threat to her femme identity, it is not because of mobility issues: "When I lost the markers of femme identity, I missed them terribly and wondered if I *was* still femme. One of the most upsetting losses was makeup, specifically lipstick."[40]

Although my story is about high heels, not lipstick, I recognize a similar dynamic as Wachsler's loss throws her into a struggle with gender identity. It is this loss-that-threatens-gender-identity that I am here calling castration. While classic psychoanalytic theory believes castration is the loss of masculinity, this lesbian femme writing suggests that one can also experience the loss of femininity as castration.

Wachsler prefaces her dilemma with a story of another lesbian confronting disability. A year before her own fall "into the deep, murky waters of illness and disability," Wachsler attends the monthly Femme/Butch Rap at a gay and lesbian health center: "I remember one woman in particular with soft red hair. She said she had a disability and it made her question her identity as butch. Wasn't the butch supposed to be the do-er . . . the one who says, 'Let me get that for you, honey?' . . . I remember thinking, 'I guess that's not a problem if you're femme.'"[41]

That last line is, of course, ironic. This recollection is the lead-in to the problems disability poses for Wachsler's femme identity. But "that's not a problem if you're femme" is also true if by "that" we mean the relation between disability and being "the do-er." While both butches and femmes experience castration anxiety in response to disability, our particular anxieties point to gender-differentiated ways of being phallic. Classic psychoanalytic theory proposes that masculinity has to do with having the phallus, whereas femininity, with being the phallus. Our detour through lesbian writing could revise that as: While femmes are phallic because of how they look, butches are phallic because of what they do.

A particularly moving account of butch confrontation with disability appeared in the 2003 special issue on disability studies of the queer theory journal *GLQ*. This remarkable text certainly echoes Wachsler's redheaded butch in her sense that the butch is the "do-er." But whereas Wachsler's butch "does" chivalrous things like "get that for you, honey," in S. Naomi Finkelstein's text the butch's "doing" is explicitly and graphically sexual: "How can I be a butch without my hands? How can I fuck when my muscles shudder as a result? . . . One of the worst things by far is that . . . I cannot feel the nerves in her cunt or asshole as I used to; I cannot move deftly enough over her clit. I cannot bend my neck to eat her out or rim her."[42]

The issue of GLQ where Finkelstein's text appears is titled "Desiring Disability." I love this title for its promise of bringing desire to the place of disability. No text in the rich, double-length special issue does this better than Finkelstein's. I am tempted to quote way too much. The opening is flat-out sexy: "She is lying on my bed, ass up. Jesus, I love her ass. She has opened herself for me. . . . I move my hand in and out of her ass, faster and then faster still. She is moaning now and opens up for me a little more."[43] That interjected "Jesus" speaks from the place of Finkelstein's desire.[44]

After two pages of hard-core description of sexual activity, disability makes its unwelcome entrance: "If it is possible to fuck her as hard as we both want . . . then I am doing just that. . . . My arm is at an angle that my neck, with three bone spurs going into my vertebrae, does not like. My body starts to shake. . . . My arm and then my hand go numb. . . . I am still fucking her . . . but I cannot feel the smooth inside of her anymore, and my neck is screaming in anguish." Finkelstein nonetheless succeeds in making her femme come: "My back is in a spasm, but I ignore it: I finish fucking her through gritted teeth. . . . She comes . . . she finishes."

Despite the detailed account of the butch's pain, the episode is sexy to read—with the exception of the final paragraph. Here's how the story ends: "While she rests, I go into the bathroom to take a muscle relaxant and to the kitchen to get an ice bag. . . . The next day I have to go to the emergency room for Toradol, a major anti-inflammatory that leaves me unable to eat for two days because it makes me nauseous and gives me the runs. But it does take the swelling down."[45]

The ending of her story is literally anticlimactic, but the ending of the story is not the end of Finkelstein's text. Powerful as it is, the anecdote only takes up about a quarter of the text. The rest is not narrative but thoughts about her life as a "cripbutch," which include not only candor about her disability but also insistence on her on-going sexuality, on her persistent desire.[46] Like Platt and Wachsler, Finkelstein experiences disability as a threat to gender identity, but—probably because her identity is butch not femme—it is eas-ier to hear that threat as castration: "How's a butch supposed to stay butch when hir body is not cooperating? I have felt emasculated by my disease."[47] As I try to think through the temporalities of the phallus here, tracing the ways that adult-onset disability affects the phallus, Finkelstein's text is particularly valuable to me.

Like Platt, Finkelstein experiences the threat disability poses to her gender identity as a repetition. As mentioned earlier, Platt's en-titling her essay "Reclaiming Femme . . . Again" frames disability's threat to her identity as a repetition of the 1970s feminist rejec-tion of femme. Finkelstein connects disability's threat to society's disapproval of butch women: "I have paid many a price for being butch. . . . Hell, I have almost been killed more than once for being a butch. . . . I have lived with all these sanctions and stayed a butch because of my fierce love for women, my need to be inside them. . . . But how can I be a butch without my hands? . . . After all I have lived through and endured—I face losing the capacity to be butch? Damn, that has to be a bad joke."[48]

I am interested in the temporality suggested by both Platt and Finkelstein. In their accounts, disability's threat to gender is a repe-tition. They experienced a similar threat before disability appeared, and their experience of the threat as a repetition allows them, in the face of disability, to, as Platt puts it, re-claim their gender again.

Both Platt and Finkelstein end their texts by proclaiming their desire. Finkelstein ends: "Nothing that they did . . . or that has hap-pened . . . not the streets or abuse . . . or being a crip . . . has killed it. My desire is still intact. . . . The beauty of desire . . . in all its rawness and untamed hope still leaves my throat scratchy and dry, and it's the taste of glory." Platt ends: "Now my femme is rising again. . . . This lesbian femme with disabilities is wise, wild, wet, and want-ing."[49] I read "rising again" as the mark of a certain phallic tem-porality, one that manifests as repetition. These stories of lesbian gender and adult-onset disability are stories of castration, but the temporality is not one where castration, when it happens, is once and for all. It is where the phallus is lost and then regained, more than once, in a repetition ("rising again").

While I have already quoted way too much from Finkelstein, there is one more thing in her story that I just have to mention. After describing in some detail the physical manifestations of her femme's orgasm, she writes, "In my mind's eye my own cock explodes as she comes, I get that much pleasure from her climax."[50] In my reading, I don't recall ever encountering anything like "in my mind's eye my own cock explodes." These eight words are pretty much exactly what I describe at the end of my story, and it means a lot to me to discover someone else talking about the cock in her head. This is surely in part why, in my attempt to understand the modes of the phallus, I so value Finkelstein.

The Phallus in the Wheelchair

The exploding cock in Finkelstein's mind's eye brings us back to the end of my story. As I said when I began these comments, I am particularly interested in the temporality of my story, in how what appears to be a story of castration can have such a phallic ending. I now see that my story could be put in a genre with the pieces by Platt, Wachsler, and Finkelstein. All tell stories of adult-onset disability as castration; all end by affirming the persistence of their desire. I want to contrast this phallic temporality with the standard one, where castration when it occurs is once and for all.

The standard castration narrative for adult-onset disability can be found in D. H. Lawrence's *Lady Chatterley's Lover*. If I delight in the surprise of finding the phallus in a wheelchair, it is surely because of the cultural resonance of Lawrence's Lord Chatterley, castrated foil to the novel's phallic hero, Mellors. The novel displays a sort of symptomatic overemphasis on Clifford Chatterley's wheeled mobility devices, manifest, for example, in repeating the same sentence almost verbatim in two succeeding chapters: "He could wheel himself about in a wheeled chair, and he had a bath-chair with a small motor attachment, so he could drive himself slowly round the garden and into the . . . park" (chapter 1); "He could wheel himself about in a wheeled chair, and he had a sort of bath-chair with a motor attachment, in which he could puff slowly around the park" (chapter 2).[51] *Lady Chatterley's Lover* works to ensure that when we think of Lord Chatterley, we think of him in a wheelchair.

In order to highlight the promise of the phallus in the wheelchair, I want to return to Lawrence's novel, a veritable treasure trove of aggressively normative sexuality. Returning to that novel, I discover an emphasis on temporality. For example, chapter 2 ends thus: "Time went on. Whatever happened, nothing happened. . . . Time went on as the clock does, half-past eight instead of half-past seven" (17). Exploring the temporal dimensions in *Lady Chatterley* will allow me to formulate the normative temporality of the phallus and will help outline alternative phallic temporalities.

Lady Chatterley's Lover is a celebration of the most normative version of phallic sexuality. When the female protagonist gives herself to the phallic man, she of course becomes pregnant. When she rejects her husband because of his war injury, it is widely and repeatedly said that it is because he cannot give her a child. Although scandalous in 1928 for its explicit sexual scenes, this novel is a paean to the superiority of reproductive sexuality.

It is definitely a pleasure for me to juxtapose *Lady Chatterley's* normative phallus with the alternative queer phalluses I have found in lesbian writing. The novel's phallic hero, Mellors, in fact expresses a particular animus for lesbians: "It's astonishing how Lesbian women are, consciously or unconsciously. Seems to me they're nearly all Lesbian. . . . I could kill them. When I'm with a woman who's really Lesbian, I fairly howl in my soul, wanting to kill her" (223). Comments like this make me glad to locate the phallus in Finkelstein's lesbian cripbutch head, instead of in Mellors, who is militating here and throughout the novel for the most normative, reproductive sexuality in the name of the phallus.

I admit to a bit of a revenge urge in relation to *Lady Chatter-*

ley's Lover. I read that book as a teenage girl in the 1960s trying to keep up with the sexual revolution. This was supposed to be liberating sexuality, and it made me feel completely inadequate. I was, to my horror, like all the women Mellors hated, not so much literally ("consciously") lesbian as not properly, complementarily responsive to his celebrated phallic thrusts. It was only many decades later, finding myself in a wheelchair, that I thought of returning to the book to look at Lord Chatterley, to wonder how his disability figured in this expression of normative sexuality. When I did return to the book, I found not only the normative view of disability as castration, but an emphatic sense of castration as a temporal mode.

The novel opens thus: "Ours is essentially a tragic age. . . . The cataclysm has happened, we are among the ruins. . . . This was more or less Constance Chatterley's position. The war had brought the roof down over her head" (1). We might recognize this as the classic modernist sense of the effect of the Great War; it is also what I am calling classic castration temporality. This is where the novel locates its heroine and its reader before it introduces any characters or action.

Soon enough, it becomes clear that while the tragedy, the cataclysm, seems general in the opening sentences, it specifically refers to what happened to Lady Chatterley's husband. In the very next paragraph, we read: "She married Clifford Chatterley in 1917. . . . Then he went back to Flanders: to be shipped over to England again . . . more or less in bits . . . the lower half of his body, from the hips down, paralysed for ever. . . . Crippled for ever, knowing he could never have any children, Clifford came home."

Paralyzed *for ever*, crippled *for ever*: "for ever" is the temporal mode here. Its other expression is the "never" of "never have any children." Because of his war injury, Clifford is a husband who cannot be a father. The effect of this, on Lady Chatterley and in the view of the book, is a generalized sense that "ours is essentially a tragic age." When the narrator says "we are among the ruins," the ruins are a generalized extrapolation from Clifford, who is "more or less in bits."[52]

This sense of general tragedy, of "for ever," is what Margaret Morganroth Gullette calls a decline story. To exemplify the decline story, Gullette quotes Gerald Early, writing about his state of mind after a gallstone operation: "I knew then, at that inexorable moment, that I had become, finally and forever, middle-aged."[53] "Inexorable moment," "finally and forever": these are the markers of Gullette's decline story, the markers of tragedy, of what I am here calling classic castration temporality.

Gullette discusses decline in relation to the entrance to middle age, an entrance understood as a tragic fall. Clifford Chatterley is, however, only twenty-seven when paralyzed from the hips down; his story is not about aging, but about the loss of the ability to walk, to be upright, and to father children. While these are arguably two different modalities of loss, my point here is that they are confronted through the same temporality, the temporality of "finally and forever," of the "inexorable moment." Like the entrance to middle age, adult-onset disability is framed through the dramatic temporality of "for ever."

While middle age and disability might be two different modalities of loss, many people in fact experience them entangled together. Gullette's own personal story is of a back injury and the onset of chronic back pain as heralding her entry into middle age. My story could likewise be read as either the beginning of disability or the end of youth. Although Finkelstein categorizes her loss as disability, middle-aging enters her account as well: "That is the difference between me as a butch at thirty and me as a butch at nearly forty."[54] On the other hand, while Early categorizes his loss as entry into middle age, he is actually describing an experience of illness and hospitalization. It is the insistent entanglement of disability and loss of youth that indeed characterizes what Gullette calls the decline story, the dominance of a certain temporality. A third strand in this tangle, I would add, is the loss of sexual potency, attractiveness, sexuality—that is, castration.

In her struggle against decline ideology, Gullette does not allow Early's story to remain in that inexorable temporality. She supplies the needed corrective: "In time Early returned to health, teaching and a prestigious writing career. Although he doesn't mention such things, he goes on to show that he did not remain utterly despairing. . . . It would probably have been truer for him to write, 'I *felt*, for that agonizing moment, that middle age was going to be a tragedy forever. I was wrong.'"

Just as Gullette insists that Early actually had a diverse and full life after his dramatically declared "inexorable moment," I want to return to Clifford Chatterley to consider what his life was like after his tragic loss. In particular, I want to look at his sexuality after his paralysis, at how the novel describes the sexuality of the man in the wheelchair.

In the last chapter of the novel, after his wife has left him, after she becomes pregnant by Mellors—thus after the inexorable has run its course—we find Lord Chatterley in the care of Mrs. Bolton. Their relationship has become increasingly sexual, although the novel shows nothing but contempt for this "perverse" sexuality. I take the liberty of quoting at some length:

> He would hold her hand and rest his head on her breast, and when she once lightly kissed him, he said: "Yes! Do kiss me! Do kiss me!" And when she sponged his great blond body, he would say the same: "Do kiss me!" and she would lightly kiss his body, anywhere, half in mockery.
>
> And he lay with a queer, blank face like a child. . . . It was sheer relaxation on his part, letting go all his manhood, and sinking back to a childish position that was really perverse. And then he would put his hand into her bosom and feel her breasts, and kiss them in exaltation, the exaltation of perversity of being a child when he was a man. (320)

The narrator expresses strong disapproval: "really perverse," "the exaltation of perversity." The disapproval issues from the perspective of normative sexuality. It is not that this isn't sexual; it is that this is a "childish" sexuality, what Freud by 1928 had famously called infantile sexuality, contrasting it with adult, reproductive sexuality. In the early twentieth century, Freud had established the correlation between perverse and infantile sexuality, and that is indeed what we see here, from the perspective of the narrator's disgust. It is not that Clifford Chatterley has no sex life, but that his sex life is not normal.

Note the "exaltation" here, the word twice repeated, and also bodied forth in all those exclamation points when the text quotes the excited Chatterley ("Yes! Do kiss me!"). Exaltation: "The state or feeling of intense, often excessive exhilaration and well-being; rapture; elation." "*Exaltation* and *euphoria* both involve a sense of extreme personal well-being, but *exaltation* is the stronger and *more elevated* term." *Exalt*, from Latin *exaltare*, to lift up, from *ex-*, up + *altus*, high.[55] "Exaltation" connotes intense pleasure but with an emphasis on verticality. That "uplift" is particularly interesting in relation to a man in a wheelchair, unable to stand up; it is also, I would suggest, phallic. In fact, I think Lawrence's "exaltation, the exaltation of perversity" points toward what I am here calling the phallus in the wheelchair.

I find this passage sexy. Maybe it's just me, but I don't think that I'm the only one. Consider Mrs. Bolton, having her breasts felt and kissing "his great blond body" *anywhere.* "Mrs. Bolton was both thrilled and ashamed, she both loved and hated it. . . . And they drew into a closer physical intimacy, an intimacy of perversity" (320–21). Although the novel portrays her as ambivalent, both sides of her response, "thrilled *and* ashamed," suggest that she recognizes this as sexual and responds sexually.[56]

The dominant temporality of Lawrence's novel begins with Clifford Chatterley's castration in the Great War and continues as an inexorable decline. As the novel progresses, he loses more and more, fulfilling the loss inevitable from the beginning, as his wife grows distant from him, cuckolds him, and leaves to have a child by another man. But this late scene with Mrs. Bolton suggests a different phallic temporality, one where the lost phallus can return in another place. What returns is not the normative phallus, the one belonging to a "man" not a child, not the phallus that can impregnate a woman, but a perverse phallus, one no less exalting. If we release ourselves from the normative hold of reproductive sexuality, we can enter into another phallic temporality, where the inability to walk or get it up or be a man does not have to mean castration forever. Where the phallus could rise again, in the wheelchair, or in the mind's eye.

The Ending (Reprise)

The butch-femme stories of adult-onset disability discussed in the "Gender and Disability" section of this chapter testify to a particular castration temporality. Gender and sexuality are threatened with loss, repeatedly. The loss, while devastating, is experienced as a repetition and thus not understood as permanent. I greeted this as a welcome alternative to the normative temporality where the phallus is catastrophically lost, forever, once and for all. Lord Chatterley's adult-onset disability, just now considered, is *not* an example of this sort of repetition. Chatterley's disability story manifests a different temporality, a third temporality of the phallus, neither castration forever nor repetition. Clifford Chatterley's story begins as a classic castration story, but, in a perverse twist at the end, the lost phallus returns in another place, in the place one least expects it. This third temporality is the same temporality found in the story from my life that opens the present chapter.

This third temporality is, as I mentioned earlier, that of phallic surprise. The phallus at the end of my story is a surprise because the narrative up to that point leads one to expect only more and more loss, only decline. That phallus at the end of my story is also a surprise because it appears in the wheelchair, in a place marked as the site of castration. This is not a repetition because the phallus, when it reappears, is not the same. Lord Chatterley loses a normative, reproductive phallus; what he finds at the end of the novel is a queer phallus. The phallus lost in my story is able-bodied and high femme (with emphasis on the "high"); the phallus that appears at the end is cripbutch.

I wrote the story to convey this phallic surprise, to transmit my revelation that castration did not have to be forever. I wrote this story because my personal experience of the phallus in the wheelchair intimated the existence of queerer phalluses and alternative phallic temporalities.

Although the story as written ends on the wheelchair fantasy, it is thus also true that the story could be said to begin there. I was motivated to write this account of my experience by my great surprise at the fantasy that popped into my head. It was soon after that fantasy came to me that I found myself obsessively thinking of how to lay out the sequence from my life that would end on the fantasy, gradually recalling earlier scenes to lead up to what would be the final paragraph.

This dominance of the ending in fact fits a prevalent view of narrative. According to Peter Brooks's influential formulation, for example, "classical narrative . . . , starting from the end as the moment of significant revelation, embraces and comprehends the past as a panorama leading to realization in the ultimate moment."[57] Brooks's idea that the narrative starts from the end and his description of the end as revelation certainly jibe with my sense of my story. While I would argue that the rest of my account is not mere "panorama leading to realization," the fact that my ending works so classically—that the last moment is not just one of several moments but the "ultimate," definitive moment—raises other issues.

While the end may make this a satisfying narrative, and while it may transmit my revelatory surprise that castration is not permanent, ending my story in that classic way brings in other aspects of normative temporality. The most normative alternative to tragedy is of course the happy ending, and my story concludes on a pretty classic happy ending, not just in massage-parlor idiom, but also by seeming to resolve all previous problems in one final, celebratory moment.

One of the readers of this story asked about "the work done by fixing" the wheelchair fantasy "as the final moment." He went on to ask if the fantasy "marked a stable and definitive overcoming" of the earlier loss or whether it "merely opened a window onto a potential affirmation of erotic power that came into and out of focus thereafter."[58] The answer to his question is absolutely the latter, but his sense that the story's ending can suggest a definitive overcoming of loss makes it clear how this ending could distort what I want to suggest about the temporality of the phallus. I do not want to replace a vision of castration once-and-for-all with a phallic forever, with a "stable and definitive" phallus.

Just as Gullette supplements Gerald Early's "finally and forever" moment with a more balanced sense of his life after his narrative, I need to add that while my wheelchair fantasy was indeed a powerful and exhilarating revelation, one I still want to convey, it did not put a definitive end to castration anxiety around my increasing disability and my continuing aging.

While the anecdote that opens this chapter counters the decline story with a surprise phallic ending, the next chapter opens with another episode from my life that takes on quite directly the normative dominance of phallic happy ending.

TWO

POST-PROSTATE SEX

THE STORY

May 2012: Following a biopsy, Dick has been diagnosed with prostate cancer. We are sitting in the office of his urologist as the doctor lays out the pros and cons of different treatments, basically either radiation or surgery. We have already decided on surgery and so are listening more attentively to its effects. After the surgery he will be urinary incontinent and impotent, at least for a while. We are given percentages for nonrecovery of continence and potency (very low chance of lasting incontinence, higher for long-term impotence). None of this is a surprise; we have been reading all we could online. But there is one thing we could not find online, so I screw up my courage to ask the doctor: What about ejaculation? This usually sympathetic man responds as if he cannot believe my ignorance: you can't ejaculate without a prostate. After forty-five years of experience, I thought I knew about male sexuality!

While post-prostate erection was a question (to which the literature devoted a good deal of space), ejaculation was not. It is in fact the prostate gland that produces ejaculation: no prostate, no ejaculation. Strangely, this was not in any of the literature about prostate surgery; nor had I come across it anywhere in my lengthy but largely informal sexual education. Dick was likewise unaware of this fact. So we were entering a future where a familiar and substantial component of his sexual response would definitely be gone.

This set me to wondering about one of my favorite aspects of his sexual response: the liquid his penis emits in high arousal but before ejaculation. I was particularly fond of those glistening drops, slippery, not sticky; they signified really intense arousal and, what's more, were like how a woman gets wet when aroused. Would those precious drops be around post-prostate? I queried the internet, repeatedly. This liquid is colloquially called pre-cum, more technically pre-ejaculatory fluid or Cowper's fluid. I learned the names as I searched the internet, and I learned that while ejaculatory fluid would definitely be no more, there was a possibility the pre-ejaculatory stuff might still be around. I really hoped so.

Dick told the doctor he wanted surgery. We had, however, already bought tickets for a family trip to Europe in early summer. The doctor thought there was no danger in waiting until after the trip, and so surgery was scheduled for two months later. This produced an extended period in which the loss of sex as we knew it was hanging over us but had not yet happened.

At first, this threat was surprisingly sexy. What had for years been familiar suddenly became rare and valuable against the backdrop of its impending loss. A sexual relationship of more than thirty years' standing unexpectedly got a huge shot of carpe diem.

That influx lasted about a month; then a sense of obligation began to creep in. We still felt we should have as much sex as possible, since who knew what would happen after, but—habituated to the impending threat—we were more and more doing it out of an abstract sense of should. As I sit here three years later, I wish I could but cannot remember whether we had sex the day before the surgery, cannot recall the last time Dick ejaculated.

July 2012: The surgery was a complete success. The prostate was removed without complication, and there was not a hint or trace of cancer beyond the prostate. The prognosis for survival was excellent. In that moment, my relief that Dick was not dying of cancer overshadowed any questions about our sex life going forward.

Dick was told not to have sex for six weeks. This was a relief: it excused us from worrying about what had become of his sexual response. One day about a month after the surgery, having regained a good deal of his overall strength, he said to me: "I can't have sex, but you can." His tone conveyed that his motivation was not altruism, but lechery. It was a rare treat not to have to think about his pleasure, in fact not to be allowed to, to have sex with another person with no goal besides my pleasure. It was clear that giving me pleasure gave him something important, a reassurance that he was still a sexual being. I have never felt so unconflicted about being selfish. I enjoyed those weeks enormously, enjoyed the sense of the importance of my arousal and orgasm to his well-being. I got off on the primacy of my sexual response.

In an entry in my journal from that time, I see that not only was I feeling great, but I was congratulating myself: "I feel like we are well-suited to dealing with all this. The fact that I've never been that into fucking means his erection is not really a big thing."

Fall 2012: Six weeks after surgery, Dick is released to "have sex." We never asked the doctor what that meant, and I've never had less sense of what that always elusive phrase might mean. Most often, when used by a doctor, it means penile-vaginal intercourse, but Dick was a long way from hard enough to penetrate a vagina. We took it to mean that I could touch his penis, could feel free to directly stimulate him. The first couple times, it was fun and exciting. We assumed we were just starting, had no expectations of orgasm for him; enjoying my renewed access to his penis, I continued feeling sexy as I had been during the weeks previous.

But within a couple weeks, things got bad. Here's a journal entry from early October (a month after Dick has been allowed to "have sex"): "I've been feeling pretty low about sex lately. Saturday we had sex, but I never got that aroused, and felt depressed for a few hours afterward. I don't know if it's Dick's continuing lack of erection, and I feel afraid to admit that to him (and to me)."

I could not quite admit, even to my journal, that my problem stemmed from his lack of erection (hence the "I don't know if"). It was not that I missed penile penetration, but that his erection had always signified *my* sexiness to me, had given me an objective cor-relative of my desirability. Without it, I did not feel myself as sexy and thus could not get aroused. I hadn't known this about myself, hadn't known what his erection meant to me, how big a role it played in my arousal; I had taken it for granted. Which was why two months earlier I could make what in retrospect seems a particularly foolish claim about his erection not being "really a big thing."

If I could hardly admit it to myself, I certainly was not able to talk with Dick about this. I felt guilty about my response to his lack of erection, felt I was letting him down, felt it was wrong for me to feel the way I did. Impotence was the effect of his surgery for which we had been most prepared. It was a certainty; it got a lot of play in ev-erything we read. The urologist gave him Cialis to take once a day, in the hope that eventually erectile function would return. The doc-tor consistently said that it could take as much as eighteen months after surgery for that return; he stressed that *only after* eighteen months should we assume permanent impotence.

While we did not know how long it would last, there was no sur-prise in the fact that three months after his surgery he did not have erections. The surprise was how much it mattered to me. I got quite stuck, depressed. A journal entry from a month later than the last I quoted: "Sex is getting more difficult, more troubling, not better. I'm finding it harder and harder to get aroused. And I worry it'll never get better." My worry here is not that Dick would never be potent again, but that I would become whatever the female term for impo-tent is—frigid, I guess, though that's not a word I ever use.

I felt I had to protect Dick from my pessimism, that it was my responsibility to save us from the total impotence that seemed to be swallowing us up. But when, after many weeks, I finally got up the courage to talk to him about what I was feeling, I discovered he was not nearly as vulnerable to my pessimism as I feared. From early November (on the thirty-third anniversary of the first time we slept together): "Sex remains quite difficult, but I'm much more able to speak what I'm feeling. And to believe in Dick's optimism, which I can't ruin. He might not be erect but he remains upbeat." A month after that: "I remain impressed by Dick's excellent attitude.

He doesn't feel castrated, feels real optimism about someday being potent again."

His concern during this period, it turns out, was not impotence but another effect of the surgery, one we hadn't been prepared for, hadn't expected. He was experiencing a real loss of sensation, had very little sensation in the head of his penis, a result no doubt of having nerves cut during the surgery. This was having a profound effect on the amount of direct sexual stimulus he was able to get.

By this time, Dick was in fact having orgasms again. I had heard for years that male orgasm was not synonymous with ejaculation, and now I was getting regular proof of that. While the fact he could orgasm was good news, I guess, it was always accompanied by the proviso that his orgasms were very faint, had nothing like the intensity he used to feel.

This made him sad and made me feel inadequate. The things I had done for years that had reliably given him pleasure and arousal did not work the way they used to. A journal entry from that time: "I had a realization that what is hard for me is that I 'don't know what to do.' Don't know how to make him hard or how to make him come. And I realized that it's my pride in 'knowing what to do' that has always been a big part of what turns me on during sex, makes me feel phallic. And the fact is that I no longer know what works with Dick, after having known for more than 30 years."

Part of the dynamic of our sexual relation had always been that whereas my response tended to be fraught, his seemed to be straightforward and relatively carefree. When we first resumed sexual activity after surgery, I was surprised and delighted to find us in a reversal: while his sexual response was tentative and faint, mine was strong and reliable. I really enjoyed that, found it heady . . . but only for a few weeks.

For two months in the fall of 2012, I was depressed and stuck around the fact that his lack of erection severely diminished my capacity to get aroused. After two months I finally confessed these feelings to Dick, and then slowly began to listen as he described his new problems with sexual stimulus. As I read my journal for December 2012, I see frequent reference to our learning to talk better about our sexual problems. For example: "Yesterday Dick and I had sex, got stuck, then spent some of the rest of the day off and on talking about where and how we got stuck. This is hard, really hard, but I feel like Dick and I are talking about sex better than we ever did before; so I'm feeling somewhat good about that. Still, I miss the days when Dick was so 'easy' sexually."

By the end of December, after a few weeks of talking about what we had been stuck in for a few months, things improved. An entry from late December: "Yesterday when Dick and I had sex, it was the first time it seemed nonfraught, organic, 'like us.' Dick still doesn't get a full erection, but I'm beginning to feel like I 'know what I'm doing,' and to be able to see and appreciate that what I do (and am) arouses him."

Part of this was a sort of "talking cure," having to replace the clarity of his prior sexual responses and the familiarity of our patterns with talk about what we did and did not feel. So as 2012, the year of his surgery, came to a close, things seemed a bit better. While Dick didn't get a full erection, there was in fact some swelling in his penis now when he was aroused. And I was learning to read this more subtle erection as well as other signs that he was aroused, to read them as signs of his desire for me, learning to respond to those subtler clues with my own arousal.

2013: While my journal has been very helpful in this attempt to recall what happened in 2012, it stops once we reach 2013. During the months when I could not admit to Dick what I was feeling, I had turned to a journal. Now that he and I were able to talk about our difficulties and disconnects, I no longer needed a journal. A gain for our relationship, but perhaps a loss for this memoir.

Every two weeks throughout 2013, Dick had sessions with a pelvic wellness therapist. The therapy, in addition to his daily Cialis, was devoted to restoring his erections, and he did daily exercises to increase blood flow and help with nerve repair. While I was in principle completely in favor of this, it bothered me whenever it seemed to intrude into our sexual activity. Dick would report that his therapist suggested we incorporate some of these exercises into our sex play. I wanted to go along in order to support his therapy, but I did not like it at all. I found whatever smacked of therapy a real turnoff; it suggested that his erection was mechanics and didn't have anything to do with me. I knew of course that his erection and the lack of it did indeed have to do with physiology, which is why the surgery had impaired it. Yet for the sake of my arousal, I needed to be able to see his erection, at least during sex, as a response to me, as a sign of his desire for me.

We tried repeatedly to incorporate this or that aspect of his therapy into our sex, but it always bummed me out. After a number of tries over a number of months, we gave up. I do not know if this failure impeded his recovery, but I do know it was crucial to maintaining our sexual connection. While in 2012 I had to learn how important his erection was to my sexual response, in 2013 I had to learn that his erection was less important per se than was my sense that it signified his desire for me, that his becoming fully erect mattered to me less than my ability to read his body as responsive to me.

The pelvic therapist's suggestions for our sexual activity were grounded in her assumption that sex meant penile-vaginal intercourse. My resistance to incorporating the therapy into our activity probably has something to do with my resistance to understanding the penis as an instrument. An instrumental view threatens my need to perceive the penis as responsive, signifying arousal in response to my sexiness. While I have spent a lifetime struggling with and against the normative assumption that sex means fucking, in this new world of post-prostate sex, my abnormal preference turns out to be kind of an advantage.

We did not need to wait until Dick was hard enough to penetrate me, until he was hard enough for me to feel the penetration; we did not need to wait until he could maintain a solid erection over the duration of intercourse in order for us to return to satisfying sex. By early 2013, sex had become enjoyable again, felt (to me at least) like sex before his surgery, even though Dick did not become fully erect. For Dick, sex was less satisfying than it had been presurgery because he had less sensation, but he was relieved and happy to know that he was able to give me as much pleasure as before. At the same time, he continued his therapy and his exercises in the hope of returning to full potency.

As we went through 2013, I was no longer particularly concerned with his lack of full erection, having habituated myself to the subtler signs of his arousal. Thus I did not notice right away that, as the year went by, he was becoming more erect and staying erect for longer. What I did notice, however, was the reappearance of that delicious pre-cum. The first time it appeared, I couldn't quite believe it. It didn't appear again for a few weeks, but slowly it became a regular corollary of our sex again. I was thrilled to feel him overflowing with desire for me again. On the other hand, to be honest, I never missed his ejaculation, preferred his overflow to be slippery rather than sticky, was happy no longer to deal with cum on sheets and clothes and skin.

In planning to write this memoir of our sex post-prostate, I knew exactly where it would begin but had no sense of when it would end, how I wanted it to end. While writing it, I began to feel I wanted it to end "in the middle," in that moment when he had regained some but not all of his erection. I wanted to end in the middle not only because I thought it more interesting from a narrative point of view, but because I had learned to be happy and feel sexy in that period when he was only ever semi-erect, and I wanted to represent my newfound acceptance. I also wanted to transmit the strange temporality of those eighteen months when we did not know, could not know, whether Dick would ever be fully erect again.

. . .

Strange Temporalities

As the last sentence suggests, I wanted to tell this story because of its "strange temporality." I decided to write up the experience and include it in this book because it seemed clearly to be both about the phallus and about temporality. The strange temporality I refer to as I end my story, the strange temporality that I was thinking about when I decided to recount this, is the particular experience of living through eighteen months when we could not know whether or not Dick would regain potency. That temporality felt peculiar, unusual: while sexual meaning during that span very much depended on a future outcome, there was no way to know whether that outcome would be happy recovery or permanent loss. As we lived through the eighteen months (a period insistently and invariably specified by the urologist), our present was heavily shadowed by a future, but we could not know whether we were in a decline story (irretrievable loss) or a progress narrative. Were we moving toward castration or toward a return of the phallus?

These alternative possibilities involve the temporalities with which the present book is concerned. On the one hand, we have the classic fall from phallic to castrated: prostate cancer as the catastrophic and irremediable arrival of castration. This is normative castration temporality, the temporality of our anxiety about catastrophes like cancer. The second alternative offers a different temporality of the phallus, one where the phallus can be lost for a time and then regained. The story takes place during a period when I cannot know which of these two temporal arcs we are in.

In this story, despite my commitment to alternative phalluses, I suffer for a time from classic castration anxiety; I am overcome with the fear that we are inevitably moving toward castration. I would want to note that it is *my* castration anxiety, my fear that *I* will be castrated (that I will never get aroused again), that is at stake in my depression. I am the one stuck in traditional castration temporality, whereas Dick optimistically believes in the possibility of the phallus's return. As if the two of us respectively were enacting the two alternative narrative possibilities as we together lived through this strange period of time.

While this time span might be unusual in my experience, it is also quite usual, in fact standard, in post-prostate treatment. Thus we find the very same, urologist-imposed, eighteen-month period in another post-prostate story, Philip Roth's *Exit Ghost* (2007). Roth's novel, a first-person account of a week in the life of Nathan Zuckerman, is very much focused on the effects of Zuckerman's prostatectomy. The second sentence announces Zuckerman's having had "surgery . . . to remove a cancerous prostate." On the second page, we find reference to the urologist-recommended eighteen-month period of uncertainty as to outcome: "the first year and a half . . . the months when the surgeon had given me reason to think that the incontinence would gradually disappear over time."[1]

While Zuckerman here is talking about incontinence, not impotence, the two are regularly paired as the immediate side effects of prostate surgery that may or may not be permanent, and they are likewise interconnected in the novel (Zuckerman is both impotent and incontinent as a result of his surgery). The two conditions are in fact so insistently connected in this novel that incontinence seems to be Roth's way of talking about the worst kind of impotence, using a figure that makes it more humiliating, less sexual, more castrating. And although he is talking about incontinence, not impotence here, I recognize the particular temporality of the "first year and a half."

Exit Ghost is set not during that first year and a half, but nine years after Zuckerman's surgery. Yet as the book begins, Zuckerman recalls that specific period: "The disorienting shock . . . had been particularly trying in the first year and a half, during the months when the surgeon had given me reason to think that the incontinence would gradually disappear" (2). The first eighteen months stand out for Zuckerman as a "particularly trying" period, as a time more difficult than the years that followed. What makes this period especially challenging for him is that during this time he had reason to believe things would improve, that continence would return. This hope of restoration, seen from the perspective of a later period when hope has long been lost, is itself a source of suffering. The uncertainty of the initial period, uncertainty as to whether he is undergoing permanent loss or heading toward restoration, is here considered harder to bear than the later certainty of loss.

At stake in this particular post-prostate time span is, I would argue, the temporality of the phallus. As the Lacanian critic James Milton Mellard says, "*Exit Ghost* dramatizes castration."[2] In Roth's post-prostate narrative, the first year and a half stands, as it does in my story, for the period in which we do not know whether we are in irremediable castration or in an arc of phallic return. According to

Zuckerman, that uncertainty is more unbearable than the familiar temporality of inevitable castration.

Roth sets his post-prostate story not in that initial eighteen-month period, but years later, where that initial "particularly trying" period is referred to as a past moment meant to contrast with the narrative's present. Yet while Zuckerman would like to be well beyond the foolish hopes and disappointments of the first year and a half post-prostate, he in fact, despite the passing years, is not. As he says in the sentence that references the surgeon-induced period of uncertainty, "I . . . thought I'd . . . overcome the disorienting shock that had been particularly trying in the first year and a half" (2). He *thought he'd overcome*, thought he'd moved beyond what he suffered in that period, but he has not.

The "I thought I'd . . . overcome" in this sentence is, as the reader might expect, followed by a sentence that begins with a "But": "But . . . I must never truly have . . . mastered the . . . humiliation, because there I was . . . in the reception area of the urology department of Mount Sinai Hospital, about to be assured that . . . I had a chance of exerting . . . more control over my urine flow" (2–3). The action of the novel begins when Zuckerman goes to New York for a procedure to rectify his incontinence. Although it is a number of years since the initial period when he was uncertain as to whether he should have hope or resignation, we find him plunged back into a hope that he characterizes as dangerous and foolish, plunged back into the "particular" tribulations of that initial period of uncertainty, but this time feeling he really should know better.

The idea that he really should know better, that his pursuit of hope and improvement is foolish, dominates this post-prostate story. By taking the strange temporality of the standard "year and a half" waiting period and extending it far beyond that, extending the odd mix of hope and loss into a moment when he knows himself to be permanently impotent, incontinent, permanently castrated, Roth's novel would seem to side with resignation, to weight the acceptance of castration as the reasonable, mature thing to do. Zuckerman knows how the story will come out, knows he is irremediable, and thus he continually deprecates the persistence of his hope. Yet despite the undoubted wisdom of what Lacanians would call "assuming his castration," Zuckerman's hope will not stop unreasonably springing anew, to his continual and pronounced embarrassment.

Exit Ghost dramatizes this conflict between phallic hope and castrated resignation. The conflict has a decidedly temporal dynamic in Roth's novel. We first see that temporal aspect in the relation between the period of the novel's action and the past moment of the initial year and a half. From the point of view of the older and wiser present, hope definitely belongs in a past era, should have been left behind years ago.

Having *Exit Ghost* as a second post-prostate story for this chapter reinforces our focus on temporality. Roth's post-prostate narrative conveys, more than anything, a striking and general insistence on temporality. This is perhaps because, as one commentator says, "This is a book about aging."[3] After announcing that the novel is "about aging," this senior Roth critic immediately adds, "and it's a book very much about time," as if implying an inherent connection between thinking about aging and thinking about time. The most obvious markers of the novel's interest in time are writ prominently, in large type: the first of the novel's five chapters is titled "The Present Moment"; the fifth and last, "Rash Moments."

The phrase "rash moments," Zuckerman tells us, is from a short novel by Joseph Conrad, which opens: "Only the young have such moments. . . . Rash moments. I mean moments when the still young are inclined to commit rash actions."[4] Conrad's novella is titled *The Shadow-Line*: the title refers to the line that separates maturity from "lighthearted youth."[5] According to Conrad, "The aim of this piece of writing was the presentation of . . . the change from youth, carefree and fervent, to the more self-conscious and more poignant period of mature life."[6] *The Shadow-Line* is a first-person retrospective narrative, an older man recounting a period in his youth, which sets up an ironic contrast between young and old at the expense of youth (the young protagonist rejoices at a promotion; his narrating older self frames it so we know the promotion will be a nightmare).[7]

The novella from which Roth gets the title of his last chapter is in fact about the superiority of the old over the young.

Yet while Conrad's short novel might represent the superior wisdom of maturity over inexperience, "rash moments" in *Exit Ghost* actually takes us in quite a different direction. After citing Conrad, Zuckerman goes on to say: "But these rash moments don't just happen in youth. . . . With age there are rash moments too" (138). *Exit Ghost* is about the rash moments that happen "with age," the "inclination to commit rash actions" that ought to belong only to "the young" but in this novel beset an old man. Zuckerman's first rash action in the novel is his decision to undergo the procedure to remedy his incontinence, and what is rash about the decision is explicitly described in terms of its temporality: "Instead of reaching a decision only after I'd had a chance to think everything over back home, I surprised myself by seizing at the opening in [the urologist's] schedule" (16). This sets the pattern of Zuckerman's actions in this novel: he seizes at things rather than "thinking [them] over," and this rashness continues to surprise him, as he expects himself to be careful and thoughtful. Over and over in this book, Zuckerman emphasizes the precipitous nature of his decisions: "snap decision" (44), made "precipitously" (29, 52), "at this batty speed" (31), to cite examples from the first chapter alone. Foolhardy precipitousness is the dominant tempo of this novel, and it is consistently associated with youth, making its appearance in a septuagenarian a temporal anomaly, a strange and inappropriate temporality.

Although the book is full of these rash actions, the passage where Zuckerman cites Conrad specifies a particular type of action: "But these rash moments don't just happen in youth. Coming here last night was a rash moment. Daring to return is another. With age there are rash moments too" (138). The reference to Conrad is spoken in dialogue; Zuckerman is speaking to a woman named Jamie Logan, and "coming here" refers to his going to her apartment, which he does, despite misgivings, because of his intense attraction to her. The insistence on temporality in this novel is very much attached to Zuckerman's attraction to Jamie. Perhaps because Jamie is a young woman (forty years younger than Zuckerman) and the insistence on temporality is bound up with questions of age.

Not only are the "rash moments" of the final chapter title directly tied to his desire for Jamie, but the other temporal chapter title, "The Present Moment," also connects to her. Aside from titling the first chapter, the phrase "the present moment" appears only once in the text, toward the end of the first chapter, where Zuckerman tells us: "Through a single, brief meeting with . . . Jamie I was . . . opening myself to the irritants, stimulants, temptations, and dangers of the present moment" (53).

Zuckerman here uses the phrase "the present moment" right after deciding to accept an invitation to go to Jamie's apartment. He had met Jamie a day earlier and was immediately smitten with her. So when he is invited to her apartment, he says yes without hesitation, despite the fact that he was planning on leaving New York before the day for which he is invited. In order to see Jamie, he drops his plan to leave the city.

In the paragraph immediately preceding this mention of the present moment (a paragraph that begins with his accepting the invitation to Jamie's apartment), Zuckerman articulates his rashness, his foolish eagerness to see Jamie, in ways that connect it to the procedure to remedy his incontinence: "The preposterous was seeping in fast . . . and my heart pounded away with lunatic eagerness, as if the medical procedure to remedy incontinence had something to do with reversing impotence . . . as though, however sexually disabled . . . I was . . . , the drive excited by meeting Jamie had madly reasserted itself as the animating force" (52–53). Shortly after having the procedure for his incontinence, still early in the novel, Zuckerman meets Jamie and immediately experiences an intense sexual desire, a desire that motivates his actions through the rest of the novel. Not only does this reinforce the connection between incontinence and impotence; it makes the novel a narrative of post-prostate sexuality.

"Preposterous," "lunatic," "madly": this passage is rife with Zuckerman's self-deprecation. What is preposterous is his feeling potent, despite the fact that he is impotent, "sexually disabled," not to mention incontinent and old. What is preposterous is his being animated by his sex drive despite the fact that he is old. As one particularly moralistic critic of the novel puts it, "Roth's septuagenarian protagonist Zuckerman clearly suffers from a lack of emotional maturity . . . refusing to act his age."[8] This critic echoes Zuckerman's self-criticism, his sense of the age-appropriateness of assuming his castration. Yet despite his self-criticism, despite the fact that nothing had reversed his impotence, Zuckerman experiences desire, feels the wild force of his libido. While he has every reason to feel castrated, Zuckerman nonetheless, against all reason, feels phallic.

In this passage Roth explicitly sexualizes the book's rash tempo: "fast," "lunatic eagerness," "drive." The rashness that ought to belong to the young is, in *Exit Ghost*, the tempo of libido. And libido ought to belong to the young. The strange and inappropriate tempo of an old man's rash moments is, in this novel, the temporality of post-prostate, post-castration, sexuality.

Pre-cum and the Coital Imperative

In the final paragraph of my post-prostate story, I say that I wanted "to end 'in the middle.'" While I was thinking there about narrative temporality, the phrase "in the middle" strikes me now for its resonance with the temporality of sex. My experience goes against the normative temporality of sexual activity; my post-prostate story, I would say, positively queers the narrative order of sexual physiology.

In an essay in GLQ called "End Pleasure," Paul Morrison considers normative sexual temporality from a Freudian perspective. Explaining the phrase he takes for his title, Morrison writes: "Perversion is distinguished from heterosexual genitality primarily in terms of its relation, or non-relation, to the teleology of 'discharge,' which Freud calls 'end-pleasure.'"[9] Citing Freud's regular use of the term "end-pleasure," Morrison infers what he calls a "teleology of 'discharge.'" Normative sexuality is teleological; sex that deviates from that teleological relation is perverse. The normative teleology of sex is "discharge," ejaculation.

The first paragraph of my story ends with the dramatic discovery that after prostate surgery men do not ejaculate. This piece of knowledge catches me by surprise, makes me feel foolish and ignorant. My ignorance puts me in good company, it turns out. For example, Gary Dowsett, deputy director of the Australian Research Centre in Sex, Health and Society, upon being diagnosed with prostate cancer after "35 years of experience working, thinking, writing and debating in sexuality and gender politics, and 25 years of working in HIV/AIDS," learns *only when he gets a "second opinion"* that he "would never ejaculate again no matter what else did or did not occur." This expert in sexual health adds that the post-prostate loss of ejaculation "was also a fact notably absent from much of the public health literature."[10]

Dowsett notes this lack of information as part of a general critique of the overemphasis on erection and the dearth of attention to the rest of sexuality in medical discourse on prostatectomy. I definitely share Dowsett's critique of the medical overemphasis on erection, and I will turn to that later in this chapter. At this point, however, because of my focus on phallic temporality, I want to think specifically about the loss of ejaculation. I want to pursue Morrison's lead in thinking queerly about the post-prostate loss of "end-pleasure." Since the post-prostate man cannot ejaculate, post-prostate sex carries on in a "non-relation" to the normative teleology of sex.

Morrison's "End Pleasure" goes on to connect this teleology of sex to narrative: "Like the well-made narrative, normative sexual activity issues in climax. . . . Like the well-made narrative, moreover, normative sexuality is end-haunted, all for its end. The perversions of adults, as Leo Bersani notes, are intelligible only as 'the sickness of *uncompleted narratives.*'"[11] Following Morrison and Bersani, I would locate my narrative preference for ending "in the middle" on the side of perversion.[12] This perverse preference manifests itself not only in my choice of when to end the narrative but in a number of ways throughout the account.

For example, the first section of the story, which takes place before the surgery, ends with my saying that I "cannot recall the last time Dick ejaculated." If ejaculation is the classic "end," then the final ejaculation would be the ultimate end, the climax of climaxes, but here it is literally not memorable. To be sure, the sense that it ought to be climactic is undoubtedly why I feel I ought to recall it even though I do not, and probably why my not remembering would merit the dramatic position of a section's final statement.

If we understand "end pleasure" not just as ejaculation but as orgasm, we can still note its displacement from narrative climax in my post-prostate story. (Seen from this perspective, the story I tell in the previous chapter has an embarrassingly normative temporality, ending as it does in dramatic orgasm.) At about exactly the midpoint of this chapter's story, we read: "By this time, Dick was in fact having orgasms again." The orgasms come not at the end, but in the middle of the narrative. They are plural, not singular, and are not recounted as events at all, but as something that has already happened: "By this time . . . in fact having."

Of all the manifestations of my preference for ending "in the middle," the most conspicuous deviation from normative sexual teleology in this post-prostate story is, without doubt, the pride of place given to "pre-cum." Soon after learning of the loss of ejaculation, the narrative opens the question of whether there will still be pre-cum post-prostate. And the story ends with the return of Cowper's fluid.

My story privileges pre-cum, expresses fondness for "those glistening drops," explicitly says that I prefer this slippery substance to sticky ejaculate. Framing Cowper's fluid as an object of the narrator's desire sets the story up for its return as a satisfying happy ending. Yet while the narrative thus has a classic ending, pre-cum is not sexually an ending. It appears "in the middle" of sexual activity, at a state of high arousal, promising more sensation and more arousal. It does not signify satisfaction or the end of sexual activity; it is not an "end pleasure." Unlike in my story in chapter 1, the narrative climax here is not a sexual climax.

Not only is this a good example of ending in the middle (if not the one I was thinking about in the story's closing paragraph), it is also an example of an alternative phallic temporality. Pre-cum is undoubtedly phallic and is, moreover, emphatically temporal. Also called pre-ejaculatory fluid, it is commonly known by its temporal modality, identified by when it appears. Only in the face of prostatectomy did I learn that it was not the same substance as ejaculate, that it did not come from the same place or by the same means. The dominant teleology of discharge erases any sense that this is a different substance, constructing Cowper's fluid as a preliminary, a forerunner. In this post-prostate story, however, we have pre-cum that is decidedly *after* ejaculation, in that it still appears long after ejaculation is impossible. Cowper's fluid has, in this case, literally become *post-ejaculatory fluid, post-cum.*

So post-prostate sex, it turns out, not only can disrupt but can actually reverse normative sexual temporality. I enjoy this idea a lot; I especially appreciate its conceptual solidarity with the disability sex movement. Not only does "the disability sex movement . . . champion nonnormative forms of sexual expression developed by and appropriate to individuals with specific impairments," but it "poses a broader challenge to the hegemonic conceptions of *sexuality* entrenched in society as a whole."[13] The disability sex movement, like crip theory, uses the perspective of bodies with specific impairments to challenge hegemonic sexuality, to reconceive sexuality in general.

This idea of a disability perspective that could deconstruct hegemonic sexuality finds a robust articulation in an article published in the journal *Cancer Nursing* in 2013. Titled "Renegotiating Sex and Intimacy after Cancer," the article reports on a qualitative study of dozens of people doing precisely what Dick and I are doing in the story that opens this chapter. "Renegotiating Sex" audaciously proposes: "Rather than the cancer-affected body being positioned as site of illness, failure or abjection, it can be conceptualized as a 'key site of transgression,' serving to break the boundaries that define sex within a narrow, heteronormative framework."[14] I love the idea of the "cancer-affected body" as a means to liberate sex from its "narrow, heteronormative framework," and I would like to think of post-prostate pre-cum as a "key site of transgression."

In normative sexual temporality, Cowper's fluid is actually preliminary in two different ways. Not only does it appear prior to ejaculation, but its purpose is normally understood as providing lubrication for coitus. It is thus understood as functioning like vaginal lubrication. As I say in the narrative, the similarity to vaginal lubrication is part of what makes pre-cum sexy to me. What happens if these lubrications are appreciated outside their role as preparatory? What happens if there is no goal of coitus? What happens when pre-cum is liberated from "the coital imperative"?

The 2013 *Cancer Nursing* article sports the subtitle "Resisting the Coital Imperative." The phrase "the coital imperative" is attributed to two articles that appeared in *Women's Studies International Forum*, one from 1984 and the other from 2001;[15] the phrase derives from feminist sexual theory. While as a feminist I had in fact been "resisting the coital imperative" since the 1970s, for someone who found herself "renegotiating sex after cancer," this imperative and my resistance took on a whole new set of implications.

The coital imperative shadowed our encounters with the medical experts, both the urologist and the much more alternative pelvic wellness therapist. It led to confusion about what was meant when Dick was told not to "have sex" yet, and then later that he was allowed to "have sex." One of the primary effects of the coital imperative is that one particular sex act is taken to be synonymous with "sex."

The major mode of our post-prostate struggle with the coital imperative involved Dick's quest to regain the capacity for erection. Dick very much wanted to regain that capacity and was willing to put in the considerable work necessary for it, even without guarantee of success. As we went through our renegotiations, I learned that I too very much wanted him to have erections again. But the otherwise attentive and sympathetic pelvic therapist seemed unable to imagine erection outside its coital function. Within the coital imperative, erection functions like Cowper's fluid: its only value is its aptitude for coitus.

My confusion as to whether or not I valued erection was itself, I now realize, bound up with the coital imperative. Because coitus was not my sexual goal, I had presumed I did not care about erections. My post-prostate renegotiations taught me that I loved Dick's erections because of how they signified his arousal. My attachment to his erections is very much like my attachment to his pre-cum: I value these signs of his arousal not for their coital instrumentality, but because I find them sexy in themselves.

"Renegotiating Sex" offers this definition of the coital imperative: "The biomedical model . . . positions . . . heterosexual penis-vagina intercourse as 'natural' or 'real' sex, with other forms of sexual activity deemed to be preliminary 'foreplay,' an optional extra, or simply a substitute if the 'real thing' is not possible."[16] What is at stake here is the privileging of one sex act—"heterosexual penis-vagina intercourse"—as "real," thereby reducing all other sexual acts to options, extras, substitutes for the "real thing." We might remark that the "real" sex act is the only one that can lead to reproduction, and that the coital imperative can be seen as the persistence of a reproductive model of sexuality in an era when sexuality has supposedly been freed of the reproductive model.

What I must remark, because of my focus in this book, is that there is a temporal modality to the coital imperative, as defined here. "Renegotiating Sex" outlines three ways in which "other forms of sexual activity" are marginalized. The first mentioned of these three modes of marginalization is a temporal modality: "deemed to be preliminary 'foreplay.'" Not only are alternative sexual acts meant to be preliminary, to precede temporally, but as foreplay their role is to facilitate penis-vagina intercourse. This preparatory role is the same as that assigned to Cowper's fluid (and vaginal lubrication and erection). Alternative sexual activities are meant to come before coitus, to lead up to it, pave the way for it, and make it possible. Following Morrison's queer Freudian perspective, we could say that the temporality of the coital imperative is teleological.

"Renegotiating Sex" continues: "The progression of sexual acts that precede intercourse is also conceptualized as less intimate . . . in contrast to intercourse . . . which represents the 'ultimate intimacy.'"[17] We see normative sexual temporality here in the word "progression" and in the phrase "acts that precede intercourse." The adjective "ultimate" not only means the last ("completing a series or process") but also means "fundamental" and "of the greatest possible significance."[18] The word "ultimate" carries a strong sense of teleology.

We find the word "ultimate" functioning in the same way in the 2001 article on the coital imperative. This article—"Defining (Hetero)Sex: How Imperative Is the 'Coital Imperative?'"—is a qualitative study of opinions on the place of intercourse in sexual activity. In that article we read: "Intercourse is the 'ultimate,' 'logical conclusion' of sex, the 'obvious' progression; simply 'the normal thing to do at the end of it.'"[19] The words and phrases in internal quotations are all spoken by subjects in this study. The article gathers together these phrases with the same theme: that intercourse is the ultimate, the telos of sex.

The coital imperative has been critiqued by feminists, disability sex activists, and advocates for the sexuality of old people. Looking at the coital imperative from Morrison's perspective, I recognize an overpowering instance of sexual teleology. Thinking about it within our concern about temporality, I see the way a number of different temporal aspects are knotted together in this concept. In "Renegotiating Sex" we learn not only that intercourse "represents the 'ultimate intimacy'" but also that it is distinguished from other sex acts in another significant modality: "The progression of sexual acts that precede intercourse is also conceptualized as . . . play or fun, in contrast to intercourse, which is positioned as a serious act."[20] Here sex is framed as a progression from "play or fun" to seriousness, suggesting a maturation progress.

The opening paragraph of "Defining (Hetero)Sex" concludes: "A 'coital imperative' . . . makes it unthinkable that mature heterosexuals could have sex without having intercourse."[21] Note the word "mature" here; the progress to intercourse seems to be entangled with a progress to maturity.

It is not that it is "unthinkable," within the coital imperative, to have sex without intercourse, but that the absence of this "ultimate" act would mean either the participants were not heterosexual or they were not mature. Or both. Morrison reminds us that "the

Freudian narrative of psychosexual development . . . construes homosexuality as a simple failure of teleology." Not just homosexuality but any deviation from heterosexuality: "Homosexuality, fetishism, scopophilia, exhibitionism, sadism, masochism: the various perversions . . . are but . . . 'preliminary stages.'"[22] In a Freudian developmental perspective, heterosexuality equals maturity, and those outside heterosexuality are cases of what has often been called "arrested development," being stuck in "preliminary stages," ending "in the middle" of the narrative of sexual development. While the coital imperative is insistently temporal, its most significant temporality may be not the succession of acts in a sexual session (perversions as foreplay), but the developmental narrative in which sexual maturation is a progress from perversion to heteronormativity.

Thus the coital imperative is not just temporal, not just teleological, but is profoundly implicated with our conceptualization of aging. In the Freudian developmental model that Morrison cites, aging means the progress from child to adult. We hear echoes of that teleological view of aging when the 2001 article connects the coital imperative to "mature" heterosexuality. This teleological view of aging is, actually, radically truncated, as it covers only the first period of aging, from child to adult. What happens if we apply this sexual developmental model to the other age class that we also call mature?

The average age of the participants in the "Renegotiating Sex" study is fifty-five years old. For many of these middle-aged or older adults, "sexual renegotiation after cancer centered on the redefinition of sex outside the coital imperative, meaning that current noncoital practices were positioned as sex."[23] Although the majority of participants were able to free themselves from the coital imperative, the normative developmental model nonetheless still could frame their understanding of sex. For at least some of them, coitus continued to signify mature, adult sexuality.

We can see this in participants' statements about their experience of post-prostate sex. A sixty-eight-year-old survivor of prostate cancer describes noncoital sex as "like going back to adolescent sex." A forty-five-year-old female partner of a man with prostate cancer referred to their noncoital intimacy as "like being teen-agers." A fifty-six-year-old female partner of a man with prostate cancer says that in their noncoital sexual activity, they feel "like a couple of children."[24] These participants connect their postcoital sex to a much earlier period in their sexual experience. Despite their age and experience, despite being post- rather than precoital, they express a sense of noncoital sex as not-adult, as associated with adolescents or even children.

Given my interest in temporality, I want to think about this "going back" to adolescent sex. In a developmental model, adoles-cent or childhood sexuality is preliminary, coming before the "real thing," but here the traffic is not one-way. Not only can one go for-ward, but one can go back, and the return can bring appreciation of what is imbued with the excitement of the not-yet-finished. What happens to our teleological sense of sexual development when we include not only a precoital but also a postcoital period?

I cannot help but think that our sense of the noncoital as pre-adult is connected to the residual dominance of the reproductive model of sexuality. In that model, adult sexuality is reproductive: coitus is "serious" rather than "play or fun" because it leads not just to pleasure but to parenthood. Yet post-prostate men, whatever they can or might do sexually, cannot reproduce (because they can-not ejaculate). Post-prostate men, like postmenopausal women, are postreproductive.

In the developmental model that privileges serious, reproductive sexuality, "mature" is the positive value, while its opposite, "imma-ture," means lacking. But, for the 2013 study participants renegoti-ating sex post-prostate, "mature" might not be the best quality to as-sociate with sex. In "Renegotiating Sex" the connection to pre-adult sexuality is definitely a plus. Perhaps because it offers a return to "play or fun." "Like adolescent sex," "like teenagers," "like children": the article gathers these statements together and comments that "this was reminiscent of a period of precoital sexual discovery earlier in their lives."[25] These mature adults find themselves harking back to a period when sex is imbued with "discovery," with the thrill of the new and unknown. Post-prostate sex is, surprisingly, rejuvenating.

Philip Roth's Nathan Zuckerman, likewise negotiating post-prostate encounters in *Exit Ghost*, also finds himself feeling like a teenager: "I could have been a fifteen-year-old boy on that bench, my mind given over completely to the new girl who'd been seated next to me on the first day of school" (99). His mind here is completely given over to thinking about Jamie Logan, whom he has recently met. His excitement and preoccupation with his desire for her have a definite age association. Feeling saturated with desire makes him feel like a teenager, and his language brings the "fifteen-year-old" closer to childhood and further from adulthood: "boy," "girl," "school."

Jamie is not the only woman in *Exit Ghost* who sends Zuckerman back in time to his youth. His week in New York also includes an encounter with Amy, a woman he met and was immediately smitten with in the first Zuckerman novel, *The Ghost Writer*, which takes place nearly fifty years earlier; a woman he has not seen since. Like Zuckerman, Amy in *Exit Ghost* is no longer young; like Zuckerman, she has been ravaged by cancer. Despite having seen the effects of age and cancer on the woman he so powerfully desired in his youth, here is what Zuckerman feels as he phones Amy, halfway through the novel:

> I dialed her number as though it were the code to restoring the fullness that once encompassed us all; I dialed as though spinning a lifetime counterclockwise were an act as natural and ordinary as resetting the timer on the kitchen stove. My heartbeat was discernible again, not because I was anxiously anticipating being within arms' reach of Jamie Logan but from envisioning Amy's black hair and dark eyes and the confident look on her face in 1956. . . . My determination to reach her had transported me nearly fifty years back, when gazing upon an exotic girl with a foreign accent seemed to an untried boy the answer to everything. I dialed the number now as a divided being . . . as the fledgling she'd met in 1956 *and* as the improbable onlooker that he had become by 2004. Yet never was I less free of that fledgling. (149–50)

I quote this passage at length because of its emphasis on the twisted temporality of Zuckerman's desire. Perhaps the image of dialing "as though spinning a lifetime counterclockwise" works best for those of us who remember rotary dial phones. I also think that "restoring the fullness" is about returning to phallic youth after castrating age. In this moment of desire for Amy, it is easy—"natural and ordinary"—to go back in time.

"Fullness" here is located not in maturity but in youth. Although Zuckerman is in his twenties when he meets Amy in *The Ghost Writer*, the youth in question here, the youth of "fullness," is lack of adulthood: "untried boy," "fledgling." A "fledgling" is, my dictionary tells me, "one that is young and inexperienced," from the literal meaning, "a young bird that has recently acquired its flight feathers."[26] For the septuagenarian Zuckerman, phallic "fullness" belongs to the young and inexperienced, to those just learning to fly.

The phallus has, in fact, a surprising position in the Freudian model of sexual development. Late in his theorizing and in his life, Freud came up with something he called the "phallic stage." This stage was introduced in a paper he wrote in 1923, the year he was diagnosed with cancer at the age of sixty-six. The stage was a late addition to his already established developmental model of sexuality.[27] The phallic stage is the last stage of infantile sexuality—after the oral and anal stages, but before adult sexuality. What is phallic in Freudian sexuality is not mature, adult sexuality, but this final stage of childhood sexuality: genital but not reproductive.

In the Freudian teleological climb to maturity, the phallic phase must be left behind in order to accede to serious adult sexuality. For Freud, the phallus is not the telos of sexuality, but something in the middle of development. In contrast with adult genitality, Freud's phallic stage is ignorant of coitus. Sexuality in the phallic stage has not yet entered the coital imperative.

Resisting the Coital Imperative

The 2013 article in *Cancer Nursing* "Renegotiating Sex" is subtitled "Resisting the Coital Imperative" because it finds that those who resist the coital imperative are more successful in renegotiating sex after cancer. The study concludes: "Resistance of the coital imperative should be a fundamental aspect of information and support provided by health professionals who seek to reduce distress associated with sexual changes after cancer."[28] The tone of this recommendation is modest ("information and support"), but its conclusion is actually revolutionary, at least in the context of medicalized sexuality. This article represents a major intervention into the standard treatment of post-prostate sex by health professionals. The standard treatment focuses exclusively on restoring erection with a goal of coitus. "Renegotiating Sex" finds that "the majority of participants who had tried techno-medical aids in order to produce or maintain an erection gave negative accounts of the experience."[29] By contrast, those redefining sex outside coitus were much more successful.

The idea of resisting the coital imperative derives from feminist sexual theory. In its critique of normative sexuality, it can also ally itself with queer theory. Such critiques are, to say the least, rare in the world of medicalized sexuality. As Gary W. Dowsett comments, "The understanding of men's sexuality that underpins the field is . . . at best rudimentary; it is as if 40 years of feminist and queer theory and activism have somehow passed urology by unnoticed."[30]

Unlike most medical practitioners, the authors of "Renegotiating Sex" are in fact versed in feminist and queer theory, and in addition to their suggestions for health practitioners dealing with cancer patients, they have an important theoretical contribution to make to the study of sexuality. As I mentioned earlier, from the point of view of their study of people renegotiating sex after cancer, they propose that "the cancer-affected body . . . can be conceptualized as a 'key site of transgression,' serving to break the boundaries that define sex within a narrow, heteronormative framework."[31] Conceptualizing the cancer-affected body this way brings a radical, crip theory perspective to sex, which is why I find this article so exciting theoretically.

But practically, I want to focus here on its implications for post-prostate sex. The 2013 article reinforces my own sense that decades of resisting the coital imperative, thanks to feminist sexual theory, had made me and Dick more able to negotiate sex after his prostate surgery rendered him impotent. While I was wrong to think his impotence would not be a big deal for me, I was not wrong to think that our relative freedom from the coital imperative had prepared us for successful renegotiation, in a way that none of our medical advisers ever mentioned.

Roth's Zuckerman, on the other hand, seems completely confined within the coital imperative. After rashly accepting the invitation to Jamie's apartment, he finds himself "thinking . . . of the pleasure I could no longer provide a woman even should the opportunity present itself" (52). Throughout the novel, while he continually wavers on what he wants to do, Zuckerman never doubts that his impotence means he is incapable of "providing a woman pleasure."

Zuckerman pretty much embodies what "Renegotiating Sex" refers to as "distress associated with sexual changes after cancer." He describes himself as "a man bearing between his legs a spigot of wrinkled flesh where once he'd had the fully functioning sexual organ . . . of a robust adult male" (109). We might call this castration. In the last chapter of the novel, Zuckerman says that "the sexual union with women had been broken . . . by the prostate surgery" (278). For Zuckerman, prostate surgery not only left him impotent; it "broke the sexual union with women." We might call this castration as well.

Despite his fictional status, I find myself wishing Zuckerman could have talked to the nonfictional Ted Allan, likewise a Jewish writer and a septuagenarian, who plays a lively role in a book on aging published in 1991. In answer to the question "But can you make love when you're impotent?" Allan replies: "I'd like to remind my fellow men that we have other means beside the penis to . . . give pleasure. . . . If two people are happily trying to give each other pleasure, they'll find the means to do so, no matter what degree of impotence the man may have."[32]

"Degree of impotence": this is not a formulation we often hear. Potency tends to be a binarized concept, the binary a symptom of castration anxiety, I would say. At the first sign of failure to achieve or maintain full erection, we fear total impotence forever. Allan's notion of degree of impotence resonates with my post-prostate story. In that story, "as 2012, the year of his surgery, came to a close . . . while Dick didn't get a full erection, there was in fact some swelling in his penis now when he was aroused." (I call this a "more subtle erection.") "As we went through 2013 . . . he was becoming more erect and staying erect for longer." Renegotiating sex post-prostate was for me learning to recognize degrees of potency.

Allan is speaking to us from another era, before the patenting of Viagra in 1998, before the "medicalization of impotence as the disease entity erectile dysfunction (ED)."[33] Between his era and ours, impotence was transformed into "erectile dysfunction." In her 2006 article "Bad Bedfellows: Disability Sex Rights and Viagra," Emily Wentzell critiques the discourse of ED from a disability sex rights perspective (what I would also call a crip theory perspective). As an alternative to the phrase "erectile dysfunction," Wentzell offers "erectile difference." Exemplifying this crip theory difference-rather-than-dysfunction perspective, she consistently uses the phrases "nonnormative erections" and "less-than-ideal erections."

Not only does the medicalized discourse of ED binarize impotence, but it serves to keep sexuality under the sway of the coital imperative. An article from 2009 on gay men and prostate cancer tells us that "some studies on erectile dysfunction, especially those concerning pharmaceutical interventions, specify vaginal-penile penetration as definitional for erectile dysfunction. Even when not specified, that criterion is often implicit in the discussion."[34] An article on the aging male body published in 2002 is even more definitive: "penile erection, the functionality of which is defined by its ability to penetrate a vagina."[35] Erectile dysfunction, it turns out, is medically defined as the inability to perform penile-vaginal intercourse.

Furthermore, these biomedical definitions of normative potency can implicate mental health as well. "Renegotiating Sex" tells us: "The 'coital imperative' . . . is enshrined in definitions of 'sexual dysfunction' in the *Diagnostic and Statistical Manual of Mental Disorders* [*DSM*] of the American Psychiatric Association, used to diagnose inability to perform coital heterosexual sex as pathological."[36] As someone who remembers the 1970s struggle for gay liberation, this account of the current *dsm* gives me pause.

The *DSM* was an important site in the battle to depathologize homosexuality. One of the landmark victories of gay liberation, the 1973 banishment of homosexuality from the *DSM* (where it had previously been the name of a disease or a disorder), signified that homosexuality was no longer officially pathological. Reading this 2013 account of "sexual dysfunction" in the *DSM*, it looks to me as if, forty years after the official depathologization of homosexuality, the inability to perform coital heterosexual sex has returned as the definition of dysfunctional, pathological, sexuality.

Longitudinal Sexuality

Philip Roth's *Exit Ghost* is not only about aging; it is also a book about medicalization. Even before the dramas created by Zuckerman's encounters with Jamie and Amy, all the action in the story is set in motion by his decision to go to New York to have a "procedure." Zuckerman chooses to have this procedure despite feeling it is a foolish thing to do—which is exactly how he feels about everything else he does in the novel, but he feels it first about submitting to the procedure. He first sees Amy in the elevator to the building where he has his doctor's appointment; she, too, is a patient, though of a different doctor. As older people, as people with cancer, Zuckerman and Amy both inhabit the world of medicalization.

Although Zuckerman's procedure is for incontinence, not impotence, the novel consistently entangles medicalization with his sexuality. It was his surgery, Zuckerman tells us, that "broke the sexual union with women"; it was, we might say, a surgeon's knife that castrated him. Zuckerman's dilemma is the dilemma of the old man in a world of medicalized sexuality. Zuckerman had his pros-tatectomy in 1995, which happens to be the moment when medi-calization transformed our culture's understanding of the sexuality of aging men.

Writing in 1995 about the rampant medicalization of impo-tence, Leonore Tiefer, who worked as a psychologist and sexologist in a hospital urology department, explains: "Medicalization is . . . a gradual social transformation whereby medicine . . . comes to exer-cise authority over areas of life not previously considered medical." Tiefer goes on to say that there are two types of medicalization: "Type one occurs when a previously deviant behavior . . . comes to be redefined as a medical problem; type two occurs when a com-mon life event is redefined as a medical problem and often focuses on the physical changes associated with aging."[37] Queer theory has focused on and critiqued the first type of medicalization. Scholars working at the intersection of sexuality and aging are drawing our attention to the powerful effect of the second type. Whereas the medicalization of deviance happened in the late nineteenth and early twentieth centuries, the medicalization of old men's sexuality took place a century later.

A century ago, according to Stephen Katz and Barbara Mar-shall, who have studied the changing historical constructions of aging and sexuality, "sexual decline was assumed to be an inevi-table and universal consequence of growing older."[38] This point of view continued through most of the twentieth century. There was, in fact, a positive spin to this decline: "Common wisdom of the 19th and early 20th centuries often praised the benefits of a post-sexual life."[39] In the common wisdom of the modernist period, "aging in-dividuals were expected . . . to appreciate the special moral benefits of postsexual maturity."[40] Postsexuality conveyed "moral benefits": there was a superiority to age; there was wisdom to being beyond passion. "A century later," Katz and Marshall go on to say, "we find ourselves in a culture . . . where these assumptions have been com-pletely reversed. Waning sexual capacities associated with normal aging are now pathologized as sexual dysfunctions that require . . . remedial goods and services."[41] In brief, the sexuality of the aging has been medicalized. This reversal takes place during the 1980s and 1990s.

In 2002 and 2003 Marshall and Katz published two crucial articles based on their study of these historical shifts in our culture's understanding of old men's sexuality.[42] Roth sets his *Exit Ghost* in the same period, in 2004. Zuckerman's dilemma in that novel might be understood as the battle between the two versions of old men's sexuality outlined by Marshall and Katz, between the model that dominated for most of Zuckerman's life and the new model that began to hold sway in the 1990s.

Over and over again, Zuckerman asserts that the path of wisdom, the path he believes he should stay on, is one where he accepts a postsexual life. While he consistently argues for the superiority of his postsexual life, he nonetheless cannot help but cede to the temptations of his sexual desire. As the novel emphasizes, this weakness parallels his ceding to the temptation to believe in medical remediation. While he constantly dismisses both his hope for medical remediation and his sexual desire as ridiculous, he continually—seemingly against his will—opts for desire and hope.

Zuckerman seems thus torn between two views of his post-prostate situation. In one view, he should accept that he is irremediably postsexual; in the other, he cannot help but feel desire. What for me is most stunning about Zuckerman's dilemma is how it could be seen to stage the confrontation between two different cultural ideologies of old men's sexuality, between the view that held sway for most of the twentieth century, and the view that came to prominence as the century closed, at the very moment that Zuckerman became post-prostate.

Zuckerman believes in the older model; it comforts him and makes sense of his life. This model undergirds his reference to Conrad's *The Shadow-Line*, published a century ago. As I've noted, Conrad's short novel is about the superior wisdom of older men contrasted with the rashness of youth. While Conrad was sure that rash moments belong to youth, in *Exit Ghost* Zuckerman learns that despite his age, rash moments can happen to him: "I was learning at seventy-one . . . that the drama that is associated usually with the young . . . with young men like the steadfast new captain in *The Shadow-Line* . . . can also startle and lay siege to the aged" (122–23). *Exit Ghost* is the story of his being besieged by something that is not in Conrad's notion of maturity; it portrays Zuckerman being besieged by the new twenty-first-century model of old men's sexuality.

At the turn from the twentieth to the twenty-first century, psychologist Eli Coleman, former president of the World Association for Sexology, declared a "new sexual revolution": "For men and women alike, aging will no longer signal the retirement of sexual behaviours."[43] The new model here trumpets itself as an advance over the old, as progress. Quoting Coleman's version of "the widely recounted progress story . . . ending age-related sexual limits," Marshall contends that "this is a problematic story that effaces much of the complexity of histories of both sexuality and aging."[44]

Marshall recognizes that the new model is an improvement. "The new discourse," she writes, "is an improvement over past views that portrayed older people as both undesiring and undesirable."[45] I would certainly not want to minimize the value of recognizing older people as sexual; that is in fact one of the goals of this book. Yet just as feminist sexual theory critiqued the "sexual revolution" of the mid-twentieth century, "recent work in cultural gerontology and feminist cultural studies . . . might mute an overly celebratory reading" of this "new sexual revolution."[46]

What the birth control pill was to the mid-twentieth-century sexual revolution, Viagra is to the new sexual revolution. In their first article on the new model for old men's sexuality, Marshall and Katz write, "If one event can be singled out as securing this view . . . then it would have to be the introduction of Viagra . . . in the spring of 1998."[47] Marshall and Katz make it clear that Viagra is not a cause but a result of the new model. Although Zuckerman is besieged by the new model, although *Exit Ghost* takes place in the era of Viagra, he does not use or even mention it. In my post-prostate story, however, Dick takes Cialis, a competitor to Viagra introduced in 2003.

Let me first say that, while Cialis further entangles us in the coital imperative of medicalized sexuality, I am glad Dick takes it. From my point of view, daily-use Cialis is better than Viagra because less immediately and directly instrumental in its framing of erections. Because Cialis is not taken in relation to any session of sexual activity, the penis swelling during sexual activity seems like a response to our interaction rather than an effect of the pill. Yet despite this preference for Cialis, I recognize that using a pill that treats erectile dysfunction has completely implicated us in the new biomedical regime of aging sexuality.

Perhaps the most pointed and most theoretically cogent critique of contemporary medical remedies for impotence is Wentzell's 2006 article "Bad Bedfellows." Because this article is one of very few that share my triple focus on sexuality, disability, and aging, I will quote it at some length here: "Viagra can be a useful technological intervention that can do real good in individuals' lives. However, this individual good comes at the cost of conceptualizing changes in sexual and bodily function that occur with age as pathological, which precludes adoption of a perspective critical of narrowly defined normative physical function, and promotes sexual ageism. . . . Adoption of the idea that sexual changes associated with aging are medical problems will severely hinder the ability of aging populations to reconceptualize aging and disability in ways that challenge restrictive norms."[48]

Applying a disability rights perspective, a crip theory perspective, Wentzell's response to remedies like Viagra is mixed. Though not opposed to individuals using it, she insists on its cultural cost. Wentzell's critique is not of Viagra or any remedy per se, but of the norms that led to and are reinforced by its discovery. The point is not, she makes clear, whether or not we should take Viagra (or Cialis), but rather what conceptions of sexuality are entailed by the pathologization of impotence.

Perhaps no one has been more involved in identifying the new conception of sexuality behind the pathologization of ED than Barbara Marshall. While Marshall is not, like Wentzell, explicitly working from a disability rights perspective, she comes to a similar verdict about the current model for old people's sexuality. Recently she has taken to calling the new model the "sexy oldie" discourse, borrowing this cringeworthy, cutesy phrase from a 2009 article by

Tiina Vares.[49] In 2012, the year of Dick's prostatectomy, Marshall writes: "The contradictory alternatives of an asexual old age, and the 'sexy oldie' discourse, do not . . . resonate with what qualitative research has found about older peoples' experiences. . . . There is an urgent need for more research that recognizes diversity in late-life sexualities, in contrast to the 'one size fits all' biomedical models."[50]

The "contradictory alternatives" that Marshall names here are the old twentieth-century model versus the new twenty-first-century model for late-life sexuality: either the old are no longer sexual or they are sexual just like they used to be, just like young people. These are precisely the alternatives Nathan Zuckerman grapples with in *Exit Ghost*. In that novel, opting for either alternative turns out to be impossible, as Zuckerman and the novel swing back and forth between the two. He can't choose because neither alternative fits his experience.

In her 2012 statement, Marshall suggests that the way out of Zuckerman's double bind would be "recogniz[ing] diversity in late-life sexualities," a diversity that is already recognized in her use of the plural "sexualities." This plural, this diversity, brings Marshall very close to Wentzell—who renames "erectile dysfunction" as "erectile difference"—and to crip theory models, advocating for the queer and the antinormative.

While I certainly share this embrace of diverse and plural sexualities, I can't imagine it would help Nathan Zuckerman. His account of his dilemma is more resonant with an argument Marshall made a decade earlier with her coauthor Stephen Katz. In 2003, just a year before Zuckerman goes to New York to see a urologist, Katz and Marshall published an article in the *Journal of Aging Studies* that concludes: "As positive aging has loosened sexual decline from the aging body in order to redress ageist stereotypes about sexual activity and pleasure . . . our culture exposes its impossible idea that people live outside of time."[51]

What is perhaps most wrong with the new sexual ideology that Marshall and Katz have termed "forever functional" is the "forever" part, the "impossible idea that people live outside of time." Our new ideal of sexuality is a denial of temporality, and thus a denial of aging. To affirm "late-life sexualities," to include the old as part of human sexuality, means to insist on sexuality as temporal, as changing over time. Atemporal models of difference and diversity (based on analogies to queer and disabled advocacy) can only get you so far. The crux of aging is temporality, and truly including aging in our conceptualization of sexuality means resisting the idea of sexuality "outside of time."

While Philip Roth hardly presents a model for the embrace of sexual diversity, stuck as he is within the coital imperative, his post-prostate story is firmly grounded in the recognition that aging is all about temporality. In *Exit Ghost* Nathan Zuckerman certainly learns that the idea of being maturely postsexual, however comforting, is impossible. But the new idea of forever functional is likewise impossible. From the first chapter, "The Present Moment," to the last, "Rash Moments," the exploration of Zuckerman's septuagenarian sexuality insists on temporality.

A hundred years earlier, in *Three Essays on the Theory of Sexuality* (1905), Freud actually gave sexuality a temporality. In order to recognize infantile sexuality, Freud had to be willing to recognize different sexualities, had to be able to expand beyond the coital imperative to recognize diverse ("polymorphous") manifestations of sexuality. His formulation of infantile sexuality thus not only includes a wider range of sexualities but also understands sexuality as changing over time. Unfortunately, his timeline ends when we achieve adulthood. Freud shared his era's assumption that aging meant the decline of sexuality, that aging was a form of castration.[52] His work on the temporality of sexuality before adulthood, his sense of the temporality of the phallus, is nonetheless a good start. Queer theorists have also begun, since 2003, to insist on the temporality of sexuality, but like Freud they have focused on pre-adult sexuality rather than the sexuality of adult aging.

If "mature" sexuality meant not just the opposite of infantile sexuality but the sexuality of those we today euphemistically call mature, we could begin to grasp the temporality of sex throughout the life course. "Longitudinal Sexuality," my title for this last section of the chapter, is meant to echo the idea of a longitudinal study.

Longitudinal studies are used in psychology to study developmental trends across the life span and in sociology to study life events throughout lifetimes. My section title is meant to call for reconceptualizing sexuality as developing across the life span.

The two models delineated by Marshall and Katz are in fact conceptualizations of sexuality over the life course, but they are hardly longitudinal. The new forever functional model simply denies temporality. The older model at least recognizes aging, but it is a teleological model, where aging is represented as a happy ending in maturity, wise postsexuality. While teleology may be a temporal model, it is a reductive one-way model that tries to contain the diversity of temporalities.

Neither model is adequate to *Exit Ghost*'s exquisite sense of the temporality of age; neither model can account for Zuckerman's exploration of sexuality after castration. My own consideration of the strange temporalities of post-prostate sex is a gesture not only toward including old people in sexuality but toward recognizing that a true inclusion of the old would have to mean conceptualizing sexuality as radically and diversely temporal.

CONCLUSION

The Phallus and Its Temporalities

This book is grounded in the experience of late-onset disability. Late-onset disability, where aging is entangled with disability, is regularly figured as a threat to one's sexuality and to one's gender. This book theorizes that threat, that impending loss, as a form of castration anxiety. Thus have we been led to return here to the oft-derided and undoubtedly problematic psychoanalytic concept of the phallus.

While the phallus in this book derives from Freudian and Lacanian theory, it has here been reconceived via the twenty-first-century theorization of queer temporality. The key to a temporal understanding of the phallus is its necessary relation to castration: in psychoanalytic theory, the phallus is conceptually inseparable from castration, but the relation between the two is not a static opposition, but a temporal one. Having the phallus means being anxious about castration *in the future*; on the other hand, one who seems or feels or is "castrated" must logically have been phallic *in the past*. Although it may seem that phallic and castrated characterize two different kinds of people, in psychic apprehension they actually represent two different moments of the same life.

The phallic binary has traditionally been associated with gender: men have the phallus but fear losing it; women lost it sometime in the past. These gendered associations have made the phallus/castrated opposition particularly offensive and led to its falling out of theoretical usage. Gendered associations have also tended to cover over the fact that this involves temporality, not essences.

In this book, the opposition phallic/castrated emerges not in order to differentiate genders but in relation to late-onset disability. In this context, castrated is a figure for disabled or old; the phallus belongs to the young and able-bodied. In the context of late-onset disability, these differentiations are patently, decidedly, temporal ones; thus the implicit temporality of the phallus in Freudian thought becomes activated and useful.

While I find the concept of castration unsavory because of its association with the inferiorization of women, I was led back to it when I recognized how widespread is our assumption that a disability arising in adulthood or the approach of old age means castration. Young people fear they will "lose it" when they become old; people disabled in adulthood can feel that the onset of disability takes away their sexuality or gender. This figuration of disability and old age as castration affects not just those of us who are no longer young, not just those of us no longer able-bodied. It affects every young or able-bodied person who fears disability or the loss of youth (and who fears the loss of youth *as* disability).

In considering accounts of late-onset disability and its effects on gender and sexuality, this book has featured a number of different temporalities of the phallus. Some of these temporalities are normative; others I embrace as alternative, queer, antinormative. The normative temporalities convey a host of debilitating effects (anxiety, depression, dehumanization, oppression). It is my hope that this book can resist these debilitating effects both by identifying the function of the norm and through advocating the alternatives.

The normative temporality of the phallus laid out in chapter 1, "High Heels and Wheelchairs," is the temporality of castration anxiety. In this temporality, the phallus is lost, suddenly and violently, once and for all. The subject is henceforth castrated forever (and also retrospectively phallic, but only in a now lost, much-regretted past). This is the temporality of able-bodied fear of disability; this is the temporality through which the newly disabled adult experiences a loss of ability. And as we have learned from Margaret Morganroth Gullette, this is the temporality through which we experience the onset of middle age as tragic loss and irrevocable decline.

In addition to establishing this normative temporality, chapter 1 also discovers two alternative temporalities of castration. One alternative, found in lesbian butch-femme stories of adult-onset disability, is repetition. In these stories castration is repeated rather than once-and-for-all, and the experience of repetition suggests a temporality in which the phallus returns after castration, to be lost again, but also to be regained again. The other alternative temporality, found in the opening memoir and also in *Lady Chatterley's Lover*, is one where the phallus seems to be lost forever (where the narrative seems to follow normative castration temporality), but then we encounter a surprise twist: a post-castration phallus. In these stories the return is not a repetition because the phallus returns *in the wheelchair*, in the very seat of castration, not despite but because of disability. The phallus that returns is decidedly queer, disabled and also crossing lines of normative gender and embracing perverse sexuality. This book offers the phallus-in-the-wheelchair as an alternative outcome for castration anxiety; "High Heels and Wheelchairs" promotes the phallus-in-the-wheelchair as a crip icon for late-onset hope and joy.

Chapter 2, "Post-prostate Sex," addresses different aspects of the temporality of the phallus. It looks at phallic physiology, the ordering of sex acts, and the arc of sexuality over the life course. In each of these various aspects of phallic sexuality, we discover both a normative temporality and resistant alternatives. The normative temporalities privilege heterosexual reproductivity as well as the normate and youthful male body. These normative temporalities convey anxiety, shame, and castration to sexual bodies that may be queer or disabled or old.

It is this particular anxiety, shame, and castration that is explored (in excruciating detail) in an early twenty-first-century post-prostate novel by Philip Roth. Reading Roth's novel in conjunction with the work of Barbara Marshall and Stephen Katz on the recent medicalization of old men's sexuality, we encounter two models of late-life sexuality. One model, the old as postsexual, was normative in the twentieth century; the other, the old functioning just like the young (thanks to medical remediation), is normative now. Both models are debilitating to Roth's protagonist, whose resistance is located in his vacillation between the two, his inability to choose either model.

By focusing on post-prostate, and therefore postreproductive, sexuality, chapter 2 engages a temporality of the phallus beyond the standard developmental model that leads from infantile to adult sexuality. The normative idea of mature sexuality enters into play here, since I query the Freudian developmental model as a teleology leading from perverse to reproductive sexuality, and then wonder about its relation to the sexuality of those beyond their reproductive years (those we today euphemistically call mature). In accounts of postcancer sex, we read about the thrills of a return to adolescent or even childish sexuality in later life, suggesting an alternative to unidirectional developmental temporality.

While the phallic surprises in chapter 1 appear at the ends of stories, chapter 2 explores alternatives to the dominance of ending, establishing end-dominance as another normative phallic temporality. Chapter 2 considers various manifestations of teleology in normative understandings of sexuality: from models of the old as mature and wise (because beyond passion), to the sense of coitus as "ultimate" sex act (underwritten by the teleology of reproduction), to the privileging of ejaculation (which Freud called "end-pleasure").

In contrast with end-dominance, chapter 2 embraces what it calls the strange temporality of the middle. A good figure for that middle is the post-prostate memoir's privileging of pre-cum, a phallic substance with a definitively temporal designation as before-the-end. An appreciation for pre-cum could lead to a valuation of those exciting moments when things have definitely begun but we do not know how they will end. While this in-the-middle temporality may seem strange in a world dominated by endings (tragic or happy), by institutionalized life courses, it might just represent the experience of being alive, being *in time*, rather than in a predesignated or normative narrative arc.

Longitudinal Identities

By extending our queer and crip theory perspectives to include adult aging, this book has insisted on the importance of temporality in our understandings of sexuality. Thus advocating for temporality, I have consistently taken up opposition to any conceptualization marked as "forever." These "forevers" appear in different guises in the two chapters of the book.

Chapter 1 critiques the idea of "castration forever," where once the phallus is lost we are in permanent, unchanging castration. However, as I say at the end of chapter 1, I do not want to replace a vision of castration once-and-for-all with a "phallic forever," with a stable and definitive phallus. From the point of view of late-onset disability and its anxieties, the more serious problem is not phallic or castrated, but "forever," the movement out of time into stasis.

The critique of forever reappears in chapter 2. Marshall and Katz have called the new twenty-first-century model of late-life male sexuality "forever functional." This model proposes a sexual ideal that is not alive and changing, but static, outside of time. A version of what in chapter 1 I call a phallic forever, this model marginalizes disability and denies aging. In the guise of curing older men's castration anxiety, it reinforces, multiplies, and profits from that anxiety.

According to Linn Sandberg, "Sexuality . . . is not static but changes over the life course."[1] At the end of chapter 2, I propose something I term "longitudinal sexuality." What I mean by that is precisely a view of sexuality that "changes over the life course," as Sandberg puts it. Sandberg has produced an important study of old men's sexuality.[2] A consideration of older adults tends to bring a longitudinal perspective to our understanding of sexuality. I have come to believe that, in order to affirm late-life sexualities, in order to include the old as part of human sexuality, we must insist on sexuality as changing over time, as radically and diversely temporal.

Sandberg (who was, as far as I know, the first scholar to elaborate the connections between queer theory and aging) goes on to say that this idea that sexuality is not static but changes over time "could be seen as a central claim of queer theory."[3] Her "could be seen as a central claim" is, to be sure, aspirational. While queer theory has not to date attended to work in aging studies, nor focused on older adults, Sandberg is here imagining what queer theory might look like if it did take aging into serious account.

I share Sandberg's insight that this radically temporal view of sexuality should be part of, perhaps even central to, a queer perspective. Queer theory has been, since its beginnings, a critique of and resistance to essentialized identities, especially to essentialized gender and sexuality. An essentialized identity is frozen in time; essences are precisely those things that do not change over time. Our understanding of sexuality should not be essentialized based on one stage of life but, I believe, must grapple with change as we age, with changes over the life course. As Gullette so boldly puts it, "Queering the whole sexual life course we might call it, because it seems a more radical kind of sexual revolution than history has known."[4]

Instead of essentialized sexuality, this book has proposed a longitudinal concept of sexuality. As I finish the book, I am beginning to wonder if, beyond longitudinal sexuality, we might try to think longitudinally about identity. This might be the broader lesson of grounding ourselves in the experience of late-onset disability. The anxiety concomitant with that experience involves not just a threat to gender and sexuality but more generally a threat to identity, the threat that we will no longer be ourselves, that we will lose ourselves (who we are, who we have been). The late-onset experience means an unexpected transition from able-bodied to dis-abled. Disability studies has taught us to treat these as crucial identities, despite the fact that the first is unmarked. Foregrounding late-onset disability involves thinking about these identities as temporal rather than essential, not as two types of people, but as different moments in one life.

I have come to believe that the transition from able-bodied to dis-abled is figured as castration because we have an essentialized notion of disability, because we have an atemporal notion of ability. More generally, I suspect that the unplanned transition from one identity to another, the unexpected loss of an identity, is figured as castration because we have an atemporal notion of identity. It may be that the prospect of a change in identity is experienced as violent threat because our general notions of identity are static, do not include the inevitability of change over time.

This book began with my realization that the confrontation with late-onset disability shares many of the features Gullette identifies in our experience of middle age. That was the moment when I realized I had to add aging to my crip perspective, which then led to the book's foregrounding of temporality. Our grappling with middle age is a lived confrontation with our inevitable temporality, with the fact that we cannot help but live in time.

Very much like late-onset disability, middle age involves threats to cherished aspects of our identity. The so-called midlife crisis is indeed an identity crisis. But, I would argue, what makes it a crisis is that our notion of identity is static rather than longitudinal.

As I end this book, I am just beginning to imagine what a more general longitudinal perspective on identity might look like, what sorts of things it might entail, theoretically and existentially. As an opening gesture toward a queer longitudinal perspective, let me close here with a glimpse of a radically different take on the effect of middle age on identity. Consider this passage from Joan Nestle's anecdote "A Change of Life":

> "After forty, femmes turn butch," we would repeat laughingly, young women in the bars. But the transformation seemed so far away, and we stood so hot in our pants, that this prediction was emptied of its cultural wisdom.
>
> Now I am in my mid-forties, and for the first time I hold in

my arms a woman who delights in her femininity . . . whose lipstick-lined lips make me melt for her. . . . She is younger than I by many years, just as the old stories said she would be. I have become our own mythology. It has happened, a change of life. . . .

Let me be butch for you; I have been a femme for so long.[5]

Nestle titles her anecdote "A Change of Life," using a common if somewhat old-fashioned euphemism for menopause. Menopause in our culture, according to Gullette, functions like castration, representing women as "suddenly damaged and desexualized bodies."[6] While Nestle's "change of life" does happen in her midforties, near the moment of menopause, she uses the phrase to conjure something far removed from castration, from damage and desexualization. This is not a story of threat or loss, but literally a story of *change*.

Here is a longitudinal view of sexuality and gender. It is surely worth noting that in this account the queer longitudinal perspective is not individual but is rather emphatically embedded in a cultural context, in a queer counterculture: "cultural wisdom," "the old stories," "our own mythology." This suggests that a move out of the normative temporality of castration will be more effective with a supportive communal and cultural context, that in order to make it possible, we need to tell our alternative stories.

I end with Nestle's evocative anecdote not to propose this as a model or a new norm, but to begin looking for alternative temporalities of identity. To get us started thinking about identity longitudinally, not by having to invent something never seen before, but by finding people telling stories of how their identities changed as they aged, alternative to timeless identities but also alternative to age-spoiling identities, to irrevocable decline, to the ravages of time as castration.

Nestle's anecdote begins with young women laughing. But in her story the "old butches" (whom she also calls "elders") get the last laugh: "I hear the old butches laughing. 'I was waiting for when you would become Poppa,' Mabel said. 'It's about time,' she chuckled." In ending with Nestle's "Change of Life" here, my point is not what sets the young women laughing, that "after forty, femmes turn butch" (although I do enjoy thinking about this). My point rather is to close this book by seconding a chuckling old Mabel: *It's about time. . . .* Indeed it is.

NOTES

Introduction

1 Robert McRuer, *Crip Theory: Cultural Signs of Queerness and Disability* (New York: New York University Press, 2006).

2 Eli Clare, "Stolen Bodies, Reclaimed Bodies: Disability and Queerness," *Public Culture* 13, no. 3 (2001): 361.

3 Rosemarie Garland-Thomson, *Extraordinary Bodies: Figuring Physical Disability in American Culture and Literature* (New York: Columbia University Press, 1997), 105.

4 Quoted in Tom Shakespeare, "Disabled Sexuality: Toward Rights and Recognition," *Sexuality and Disability* 18, no. 3 (2000): 163.

5 Riva Lehrer, "Golem Girl Gets Lucky," in *Sex and Disability*, ed. Robert McRuer and Anna Mollow (Durham, NC: Duke University Press, 2012), 234.

6 I take the phrase "disability sex rights movement" from Emily Wentzell, "Bad Bedfellows: Disability Sex Rights and Viagra," *Bulletin of Science, Technology and Society* 26, no. 5 (2006): 371.

7 Wentzell, "Bad Bedfellows," 371. Wentzell cites an article by Carol Gill: "A Psychological View of Disability Culture," *Disability Studies Quarterly* 15, no. 4 (1995): 16–19.

8 Barbara Faye Waxman and Carol J. Gill, "Sexuality and Disability: Misstate of the Arts," *Journal of Sex Research* 33, no. 3 (1996): 267, 268.

9 Shakespeare, "Disabled Sexuality," 162–63.

10 Shakespeare, "Disabled Sexuality," 163.

11 Jane M. Ussher, Janette Perz, Emilee Gilbert, W. K. Tim Wong, and Kim Hobbs, "Renegotiating Sex and Intimacy after Cancer: Resisting the Coital Imperative," *Cancer Nursing* 36, no. 6 (2013): 460. The phrase "key site of transgression" is taken from Simon J. Williams, "Bodily Dys-Order: Desire, Excess and the Transgression of Corporeal Boundaries," *Body and Society* 4, no. 2 (1998): 59–82.

12 Waxman and Gill, "Sexuality and Disability," 268; Shakespeare, "Disabled Sexuality," 163.

13 Michael Bérubé, "Afterword," in *Disability Studies: Enabling the Humanities*, ed. Sharon Snyder, Brenda Jo Brueggemann, and Rosemarie Garland-Thomson (New York: Modern Language Association, 2002), 339. Bérubé was one of the panelists for the 2014 "Age and/as Disability" session, although this quote is taken from a text published a decade earlier.

14 Margaret Morganroth Gullette, *Agewise: Fighting the New Ageism in America* (Chicago: University of Chicago Press, 2011), 77.

15 Lehrer, "Golem Girl Gets Lucky," 234, emphasis added.

16 Barbara L. Marshall and Stephen Katz, "Forever Functional: Sexual Fitness and the Ageing Male Body," *Body and Society* 8, no. 4 (2002): 43.

17 Linn Sandberg, "The Old, the Ugly and the Queer: Thinking Old Age in Relation to Queer Theory," *Graduate Journal of Social Science* 5, no. 2 (2008): 118. Sandberg has since published her doctoral thesis as *Getting Intimate: A Feminist Analysis of Old Age, Masculinity and Sexuality* (Linköping, Sweden: Linköping University, 2011), an excellent qualitative study of old men's sexuality that intersects with a number of points in chapter 2.

18 Gullette, *Agewise*, 143.

19 For a good cross section of this trend, see Elizabeth Freeman, ed., "Queer Temporalities," special issue, *GLQ: A Journal of Lesbian and Gay Studies* 13, nos. 2–3 (2007).

20 Sandberg, "The Old, the Ugly and the Queer," 135.

21 Maria T. Brown, "LGBT Aging and Rhetorical Silence," *Sexuality Research and Social Policy: Journal of NSRC* 6, no. 4 (2009): 71–72. Brown discusses two queer temporality texts from 2005: Halberstam's book *In a Queer Time and Place: Transgender Bodies, Subcultural Lives, Sexual Cultures* (New York: New York University Press), and Freeman's article "Time Binds, or, Erotohistoriography," *Social Text* 23, nos. 3–4: 57–68. In 2010 Freeman also published a book titled *Time Binds: Queer Temporalities, Queer Histories* (Durham, NC: Duke University Press). Sandberg's 2008 article cites Halberstam's 2005 book as the source of her understanding of queer temporalities.

22 Janet Z. Giele and Glen H. Elder Jr., eds., *Methods of Life Course Research: Qualitative and Quantitative Approaches* (Thousand Oaks, CA: Sage, 1998).

23 Halberstam, *In a Queer Time and Place*, 2.

24 Brown, "LGBT Aging and Rhetorical Silence," 72.

25 Cynthia Port, "No Future? Aging, Temporality, History, and Reverse Chronologies," *Occasion: Interdisciplinary Studies in the Humanities* 4 (2012): 2. Sandberg likewise embraced the value of queer temporality for aging in her 2008 article, although she did not devote much time to the topic.

26 Stephen M. Barber and David L. Clark, "Queer Moments: The Performative Temporalities of Eve Kosofsky Sedgwick," in *Regarding Sedgwick: Essays on Queer Culture and Critical Theory*, ed. Stephen M. Barber and David L. Clark (Abingdon, UK: Routledge, 2002), 1–54.

27 Jane Gallop, *The Deaths of the Author: Reading and Writing in Time* (Durham, NC: Duke University Press, 2011). See especially chapter 3, "The Queer Temporality of Writing."

28 Margaret Morganroth Gullette, "Midlife Discourses in the Twentieth-Century United States: An Essay on the Sexuality, Ideology, and Politics of 'Middle-Ageism,'" in *Welcome to Middle Age! (And Other Cultural Fictions)*, ed. Richard A. Shweder (Chicago: University of Chicago Press, 1998), 32.

29 Port's was the first thing I read that looked at queer temporality from the viewpoint of aging studies; as I continued my reading in aging studies, I discovered the other texts discussed in this section. In addition to the handful of scholars cited here, I have just become aware of an article published in 2017 that uses a combined aging and queer temporality framework: Linda M. Hess, "'My Whole Life I've Been Dressing Up Like a Man': Negotiations of Queer Aging and Queer Temporality in the TV Series *Transparent*," *European Journal of American Studies* 11, no. 3 (2017): 1–19. This new article, taken from Hess's doctoral dissertation, draws easily from both aging studies and queer temporality and suggests that perhaps more scholars of aging may be beginning to use queer temporality theory.

30 Lee Edelman, *No Future: Queer Theory and the Death Drive* (Durham, NC: Duke University Press, 2004).

31 Port, "No Future?," 3.

32 Gullette, *Agewise*, 143.

33 Margaret Morganroth Gullette, *Declining to Decline: Cultural Combat and the Politics of the Midlife* (Charlottesville: University Press of Vir-

ginia, 1997), and Margaret Morganroth Gullette, *Aged by Culture* (Chicago: University of Chicago Press, 2004).

34 Port, "No Future?," 5.

35 Gullette, *Declining to Decline*, 159–77.

36 Leerom Medovoi also chooses Gullette's work as the age theory most amenable to queer temporality: "Age Trouble: A Timely Subject in American Literary and Cultural Studies," *American Literary History* 22, no. 3 (2010): 657–72. This review essay by Medovoi (who works in neither queer theory nor age studies but seems to be familiar with both) is the earliest text that I know of to connect Gullette's idea of decline and queer temporality. Unlike Gullette's work, however, Medovoi's article is concerned not with old or even middle age but with adolescence, thus perpetuating queer theory's exclusive interest in applying nonnormative temporality to the young.

37 Gullette, *Declining to Decline*, 48, 50.

38 For a book that does think about crip temporality, though not about aging, see Alison Kafer, *Feminist, Queer, Crip* (Bloomington: Indiana University Press, 2013).

39 Shakespeare, "Disabled Sexuality," 163.

40 Wentzell, "Bad Bedfellows," 375.

41 Jane Gallop, *The Daughter's Seduction: Feminism and Psychoanalysis* (Ithaca, NY: Cornell University Press, 1982), 66. See also Jane Gallop, *Reading Lacan* (Ithaca, NY: Cornell University Press, 1985), and Jane Gallop, *Thinking through the Body* (New York: Columbia University Press, 1987).

42 The first version of this debate started in the late 1920s and involved Freud and other psychoanalysts such as Karen Horney, Helene Deutsch, and Ernest Jones. Freud himself named the position critical of the phallus in this debate "feminist."

43 Jacques Lacan, "The Signification of the Phallus," in *Écrits: A Selection*, trans. Alan Sheridan (New York: Norton, 1977), 282.

44 For this argument, see Jane Gallop, "Phallus/Penis: Same Difference," in *Thinking through the Body*, 124–33.

45 Kathleen Woodward, *Aging and Its Discontents: Freud and Other Fictions* (Bloomington: Indiana University Press, 1991), 44.

46 Woodward, *Aging and Its Discontents*, 198n21: "Several important subjects go undiscussed in this book, including sexuality." There are a few tantalizing exceptions to this absence; see, for example, p. 52.

47 Woodward, *Aging and Its Discontents*, 36, quoting Jacques Lacan, "Tuche and Automaton," in *The Four Fundamental Concepts of Psychoanalysis*, trans. Alan Sheridan (New York: Norton, 1978), 64.

48 Woodward, *Aging and Its Discontents*, 37.

49 Woodward, *Aging and Its Discontents*, 1. This is the first paragraph of the book.

50 Between the two sentences that I quoted earlier from p. 37 of Woodward's *Aging and Its Discontents*, sentences that both connect "infirm old age" with "castration," is a sentence where Woodward alludes to and cites Gullette's first book, *Safe at Last in the Middle Years: The Invention of the Midlife Progress Novel* (Berkeley: University of California Press, 1988; BackinPrint edition, New York: Authors Guild, 2000).

51 Gullette, *Safe at Last in the Middle Years* (2000), 2, quoting John Updike, *Couples* (New York: Knopf, 1968), 241–42.

52 Gullette, "Midlife Discourses in the Twentieth-Century United States," 25.

53 Gullette, *Agewise*, 95.

54 "Menopause discourse still makes it seem . . . as if only women age. But men who accept the belief in midlife decline and deference to the cult of youth can be moved not only to self-consciousness about erections but lured to testosterone, Viagra, and trophy wives" (Gullette, *Agewise*, 95).

55 Lacan, "Signification of the Phallus," 288.

56 Jan Campbell, *Arguing with the Phallus: Feminist, Queer and Postcolonial Theory* (London: Zed Books, 2000), 146.

57 Teresa de Lauretis, *The Practice of Love: Lesbian Sexuality and Perverse Desire* (Bloomington: Indiana University Press, 1994); Judith Butler, "The Lesbian Phallus and the Morphological Imaginary," in *Bodies That Matter: On the Discursive Limits of "Sex"* (Abingdon, UK: Routledge, 1993), 57–92; originally published as Judith Butler, "The Lesbian Phallus and the Morphological Imaginary," *differences* 4, no. 1 (1992): 133–71.

58 Most accounts of the history of queer theory trace the phrase to Teresa de Lauretis, "Queer Theory: Lesbian and Gay Sexualities. An Introduction," *differences* 3, no. 2, (1991): iii.

59 In these early 1990s texts, each refers to the other's work.

60 De Lauretis, *The Practice of Love*, 231. De Lauretis is citing the 1992 version of Butler's text, in which "Phallus" is always capitalized. In the 1993 version of Butler's text, "phallus" is no longer capitalized.

61 Campbell, *Arguing with the Phallus*, 147.

62 Campbell, *Arguing with the Phallus*, 151.

63 Lili Hsieh, "A Queer Sex, or, Can Feminism and Psychoanalysis Have Sex without the Phallus," *Feminist Review*, no. 102 (2012): 101. While the "query" here is definitely a critique, note the wordplay.

64 Hsieh, "A Queer Sex," 98.

65 Hsieh, "A Queer Sex," 102.

66 Hsieh, "A Queer Sex," 104.

67 Hsieh, "A Queer Sex," 105, citing Tavia Nyong'o, "Lady Gaga's Lesbian Phallus," *Bully Bloggers*, March 16, 2010, bullybloggers.wordpress.com /2010/03/16/lady-gagas-lesbian-phallus-2.

68 When I say "maybe it's just me," it is not only because I find the idea of a lesbian phallus sexy, but because Butler actually says something about me parenthetically in the essay that sets my heart aflutter: "As Jane Gallop has argued (to cite her is perhaps to transfer the phallus from him [Lacan] to her . . .)" (Butler, "Lesbian Phallus" [1993], 82).

69 Butler, "Lesbian Phallus" (1993), 28.

70 Butler, "Lesbian Phallus" (1993), 262n26, 84.

71 Butler, "Lesbian Phallus" (1993), 73.

72 Butler, "Lesbian Phallus" (1993), 88.

73 Campbell misses the fact that Butler roots her phallus in lesbian prac- tice: "The lesbian phallus," Campbell writes, "works by . . . symboliz- ing other body parts . . . for example, the breast or the clitoris" (Camp- bell, *Arguing with the Phallus*, 150). Campbell lists classically female sexual parts; these two examples in fact never appear in Butler's text.

74 Butler, "Lesbian Phallus" (1993), 85.

75 For Butler's discussion of the prohibitions and the shame, see Butler, "Lesbian Phallus" (1993), 85–87.

76 Butler, "Lesbian Phallus" (1993), 262n26.

77 Hsieh, "A Queer Sex," 104.

78 Jane Gallop, *Anecdotal Theory* (Durham, NC: Duke University Press, 2002), 2.

79 Cynthia Franklin, *Academic Lives: Memoir, Cultural Theory, and the Uni- versity Today* (Athens: University of Georgia Press, 2009), 198.

80 Franklin, *Academic Lives*, 205.

81 Franklin, *Academic Lives*, 24. While Franklin shares my sense of the value of combining personal writing with theory, she does not recog- nize that I was trying to do just that in my writing from the period.

82 Gallop, *Anecdotal Theory*, 11.

83 Gallop, *Anecdotal Theory*, 6–7.

84 "Can be," though certainly not always or necessarily.

85 See Sigmund Freud, "Three Essays on the Theory of Sexuality," trans. James Strachey, in *The Standard Edition of the Complete Psychological Works of Sigmund Freud*, ed. James Strachey, vol. 7 (London: Hogarth, 1961), 125–231.

86 For example, see Robert McRuer and Abby L. Wilkerson, eds., "Queer Theory Meets Disability Studies," special issue, *GLQ: A Journal of Les-

bian and Gay Studies 9, nos. 1–2 (2003), and Robert McRuer and Anna Mollow, eds., *Sex and Disability* (Durham, NC: Duke University Press, 2012). Crip anecdotal theory seems to be part of a more general trend to include personal writing in disability theorizing. Franklin, for example, follows her chapter on feminist memoirs with a chapter on memoir writing in disability studies where she remarks: "Including discussion of [one's] own experience with disability is in keeping with the theoretical positions of disability studies scholars" (Franklin, *Academic Lives*, 218).

87 Abby Wilkerson, "Slipping," in *Gay Shame*, ed. David M. Halperin and Valerie Traub (Chicago: University of Chicago Press, 2009), 188–91.

88 Gallop, *Anecdotal Theory*, 16.

89 Eli Clare, *Exile and Pride: Disability, Queerness and Liberation*, Classics edition (Boston: South End, 2009).

90 Gallop, *Anecdotal Theory*, 16.

One. High Heels and Wheelchairs

1 Margaret Morganroth Gullette, *Declining to Decline: Cultural Combat and the Politics of the Midlife* (Charlottesville: University Press of Virginia, 1997), 48–50.

2 Gullette, *Declining to Decline*, 54–55.

3 Eliza Chandler, "Sidewalk Stories: The Troubling Task of Identification," *Disability Studies Quarterly* 30, nos. 3–4 (2010): n.p.

4 David M. Halperin and Valerie Traub, "Beyond Gay Pride," in *Gay Shame*, ed. David M. Halperin and Valerie Traub (Chicago: University of Chicago Press, 2009), 3–4.

5 Riva Lehrer, "Golem Girl Gets Lucky," in *Sex and Disability*, ed. Robert McRuer and Anna Mollow (Durham, NC: Duke University Press, 2012), 234.

6 *Collins English Dictionary—Complete and Unabridged* (New York: HarperCollins, 2014), accessed February 28, 2018, http://www.thefree dictionary.com/catwalk.

7 Lehrer, "Golem Girl Gets Lucky," 234.

8 Lehrer, "Golem Girl Gets Lucky," 234–36.

9 Lehrer, "Golem Girl Gets Lucky," 236, 234. Lehrer transmits the "S-curves" of the normative female body here with an *s*-filled sentence ("She should sway . . . spine strung . . . sinuous rosary").

10 Lehrer, "Golem Girl Gets Lucky," 234.

11 Lehrer, "Golem Girl Gets Lucky," 234.

12 Lehrer, "Golem Girl Gets Lucky," 236, 234.

13 Lehrer, "Golem Girl Gets Lucky," 236.

14   Lehrer, "Golem Girl Gets Lucky," 234.

15   "Silver Bells," accessed February 28, 2018, http://www.41051.com /xmaslyrics/silverbells.html.

16   Russell W. Belk, "Shoes and Self," *Advances in Consumer Research* 30 (2003): 33.

17   Valerie Steele, *Shoes: A Lexicon of Style* (London: Scriptum Editions, 1998), 8.

18   Lorraine Gamman, "Self-Fashioning, Gender Display, and Sexy Girl Shoes: What's at Stake—Female Fetishism or Narcissism?," in *Footnotes: On Shoes*, ed. Shari Benstock and Suzanne Ferriss (New Brunswick, NJ: Rutgers University Press, 2001), 95–96.

19   Gamman, "Self-Fashioning," 96–97, emphasis added.

20   For a good overview of the relation between '70s feminism and '90s feminism, see Astrid Henry, *Not My Mother's Sister: Generational Conflict and Third-Wave Feminism* (Bloomington: Indiana University Press, 2004).

21   Gamman, "Self-Fashioning," 98.

22   She goes on to specify that she "developed a penchant for black suede hybrid shoe-sneakers (known as 'Merrills')" (Gamman, "Self-Fashioning," 98).

23   Gamman found these quotations in Steele, *Shoes*, 16, 27.

24   Claudia Wobovnik, "These Shoes Aren't Made for Walking: Rethinking High-Heeled Shoes as Cultural Artifacts," *Visual Culture and Gender* 8 (2013): 85.

25   Gamman, "Self-Fashioning," 96.

26   The punctuation in this passage is itself questionable: the parenthesis should end after "phallic" and before "women."

27   Gamman, "Self-Fashioning," 101.

28   William A. Rossi, *The Sex Life of the Foot and the Shoe* (New York: Saturday Review Press / E. P. Dutton, 1976), 119.

29   Rossi, *Sex Life of the Foot and the Shoe*, 189, citing Lars Ullerstam, *The Erotic Minorities* (New York: Grove Press, 1966).

30   Rossi, *Sex Life of the Foot and the Shoe*, 134.

31   Wobovnik, "These Shoes Aren't Made for Walking," 87.

32   Rossi, *Sex Life of the Foot and the Shoe*, 131.

33   In my narrative, women's shoes are in fact blamed by the overbearing orthopedic surgeon. As predicted by Rossi's "female psychology," I resent the doctor's authority and his lack of understanding for my relation to shoes. Does the loss of my sexy shoes feel like castration because I understand this authority as taking them away from me? In the classic Freudian understanding, castration is imagined as punishment by a parental authority for unsanctioned phallic presumption.

34 Gamman, "Self-Fashioning," 95–96, citing Susan Brownmiller, *Femininity* (London: Grafton Books, 1986), 144–45.

35 Eli Clare, *Exile and Pride: Disability, Queerness and Liberation*, Classics edition (Boston: South End, 2009), 130. The first edition of *Exile and Pride* was published in 1999.

36 Lehrer, "Golem Girl Gets Lucky," 242.

37 Mary Frances Platt, "Reclaiming Femme . . . Again," in *The Persistent Desire: A Femme-Butch Reader*, ed. Joan Nestle (New York: Alyson, 1992), 388–89.

38 Platt, "Reclaiming Femme . . . Again," 388.

39 Platt, "Reclaiming Femme . . . Again," 389.

40 Sharon Wachsler, "Still Femme," in *Restricted Access: Lesbians on Disability*, ed. Victoria Brownworth and Susan Raffo (Seattle: Seal Press, 1999), 111.

41 Wachsler, "Still Femme," 110–11.

42 S. Naomi Finkelstein, "The Only Thing You Have to Do Is Live," *GLQ: A Journal of Lesbian and Gay Studies* 9, nos. 1–2 (2003): 310–12.

43 Finkelstein, "The Only Thing," 307–8.

44 If I draw attention to her "Jesus," I should note that Finkelstein identifies as Jewish in the text.

45 Finkelstein, "The Only Thing," 308–9.

46 *The Persistent Desire* is the title of the anthology in which Platt's essay appeared. Joan Nestle, the anthology's editor, uses the phrase to refer to lesbian butch-femme sexuality. I like the phrase here for its temporality and thus use it to mark the debt this project owes late twentieth-century lesbian butch-femme for theorizing alternative phallic temporalities.

47 Finkelstein, "The Only Thing," 311.

48 Finkelstein, "The Only Thing," 309–10.

49 Finkelstein, "The Only Thing," 319; Platt, "Reclaiming Femme . . . Again," 389.

50 Finkelstein, "The Only Thing," 309.

51 D. H. Lawrence, *Lady Chatterley's Lover* (New York: Bantam Classic, 2007), 1–2, 13. Subsequent references to this edition are given in parentheses in the text.

52 Lord Chatterley "more or less in bits" could connect to the Lacanian "body in bits and pieces," which Judith Butler reads as an image of castration. See Judith Butler, "The Lesbian Phallus and the Morphological Imaginary," *differences* 4, no. 1 (1992): 133–71.

53 Gullette, *Declining to Decline*, 172, quoting Gerald Early, "Black Men and Middle Age," *Hungry Mind Review* 46, no. 1 (1993): 26.

54 Finkelstein, "The Only Thing," 317.

55 *American Heritage Dictionary of the English Language* (Boston: American Heritage, 1969), 456, 413, emphasis added to "more elevated."

56 This "thrilled and ashamed" reminds me of the ambivalent response to Butler's lesbian phallus, which in the introduction I characterized as wrong and thrilling and which Butler characterizes both as alluring and as a source of shame. Perhaps this ambivalent mixture might characterize the relation to the perverse, the queer phallus.

57 Peter Brooks, *Reading for the Plot: Design and Intention in Narrative* (Cambridge, MA: Harvard University Press, 1992), 52.

58 Lee Edelman, reader's report for Duke University Press, 2015. I am grateful to Lee for this insight and for his evocative formulation.

Two. Post-prostate Sex

1 Philip Roth, *Exit Ghost* (New York: Vintage, 2007), 1–2. Subsequent references to this edition are given in parentheses in the text.

2 James Milton Mellard, "Gifts Reserved for Age: A Lacanian Study of Comedy in Philip Roth's *Exit Ghost*," *Acta Scientarum, Language and Culture* 32, no. 1 (2010): 17.

3 Alan Cooper, speaking in "Zuckerman Unsound? A Roundtable Discussion on Philip Roth's *Exit Ghost*," ed. Derek Parker Royal, *Philip Roth Studies* 5, no. 1 (2009): 19.

4 *Exit Ghost*, 137–38, citing the first page of Joseph Conrad, *The Shadow-Line*.

5 Joseph Conrad, *Selected Literary Criticism and "The Shadow-Line,"* ed. Allan Ingram (London: Methuen, 1986), 194.

6 Joseph Conrad, "Author's Note," in *Selected Literary Criticism*, 112.

7 I am interested to note that Conrad's narrative, like my story here, includes passages from the protagonist's journal, to capture what he felt at the time of the events.

8 Gurumurthy Neelakantan, "Fiction as Faith: Philip Roth's Testament in *Exit Ghost*," *Philip Roth Studies* 10, no. 2 (2014): 43n6.

9 Paul Morrison, "End Pleasure," *GLQ: A Journal of Lesbian and Gay Studies* 1, no. 1 (1993): 55, citing Sigmund Freud, *Three Essays on the Theory of Sexuality*.

10 Gary W. Dowsett, "'Losing My Chestnut': One Gay Man's Wrangle with Prostate Cancer," *Reproductive Health Matters* 16, no. 32 (2008): 145–46.

11 Morrison, "End Pleasure," 55, quoting Leo Bersani, *The Freudian Body* (New York: Columbia University Press, 1986), 32.

12 Those interested in narrative pleasure and temporality might want to connect this not just to Bersani and Morrison but also to recent cri-

tiques of the normativity of narrative end-pleasure. For example, in the 2013 collection *Narrative Middles*, Amy M. King writes that "normative narrative theories" understand "the reader's desire . . . as desire for conclusion." King goes on to explore "a different kind of [readerly] desire, one . . . not based in the headlong thrust towards closure." See Amy M. King, "Dilatory Description and the Pleasures of Accumulation," in *Narrative Middles*, ed. Caroline Levine and Mario Ortiz-Robles (Columbus: Ohio State University Press, 2013), 162–63, 172, 189n6.

13 Emily Wentzell, "Bad Bedfellows: Disability Sex Rights and Viagra," *Bulletin of Science, Technology and Society* 26, no. 5 (2006): 371.

14 Jane M. Ussher, Janette Perz, Emilee Gilbert, W. K. Tim Wong, and Kim Hobbs, "Renegotiating Sex and Intimacy after Cancer: Resisting the Coital Imperative," *Cancer Nursing* 36, no. 6 (2013): 460. The phrase "key site of transgression" is taken from Simon J. Williams, "Bodily Dys-Order: Desire, Excess and the Transgression of Corporeal Boundaries," *Body and Society* 4, no. 2 (1998).

15 Margaret Jackson, "Sex Research and the Construction of Sexuality: A Tool of Male Supremacy?," *Women's Studies International Forum* 7, no. 1 (1984): 43–51; Kathryn McPhillips, Virginia Braun, and Nicola Gavey, "Defining (Hetero)Sex: How Imperative Is the 'Coital Imperative'?," *Women's Studies International Forum* 24, no. 2 (2001): 229–40.

16 Ussher et al., "Renegotiating Sex," 455.

17 Ussher et al., "Renegotiating Sex," 455.

18 *American Heritage Dictionary of the English Language* (Boston: American Heritage, 1969), 1391.

19 McPhillips et al., "Defining (Hetero)Sex," 233.

20 Ussher et al., "Renegotiating Sex," 455.

21 McPhillips et al., "Defining (Hetero)Sex," 229.

22 Morrison, "End Pleasure," 55, quoting Freud, *Three Essays*.

23 Ussher et al., "Renegotiating Sex," 457.

24 Ussher et al., "Renegotiating Sex," 457.

25 Ussher et al., "Renegotiating Sex," 457.

26 *American Heritage Dictionary of the English Language*, 501.

27 Sigmund Freud, "The Infantile Genital Organization: An Interpolation into the Theory of Sexuality," trans. Joan Riviere, in *The Standard Edition of the Complete Psychological Works of Sigmund Freud*, ed. James Strachey, vol. 19 (London: Hogarth, 1961), 141–48.

28 Ussher et al., "Renegotiating Sex," 455.

29 Ussher et al., "Renegotiating Sex," 459.

30 Dowsett, "'Losing My Chestnut,'" 150.

31 Ussher et al., "Renegotiating Sex," 460.

32 Quoted in Merrily Weisbord, *Our Future Selves: Love, Life, Sex, and Aging* (Berkeley, CA: North Atlantic Books, 1991), 85.

33 Wentzell, "Bad Bedfellows," 370.

34 Marysol Asencio, Thomas Blank, Lara Descartes, and Ashley Crawford, "The Prospect of Prostate Cancer: A Challenge for Gay Men's Sexualities as They Age," *Sexuality Research and Social Policy* 6, no. 4 (2009): 39.

35 Barbara L. Marshall and Stephen Katz, "Forever Functional: Sexual Fitness and the Ageing Male Body," *Body and Society* 8, no. 4 (2002): 44.

36 Ussher et al., "Renegotiating Sex," 455.

37 Leonore Tiefer, *Sex Is Not a Natural Act and Other Essays* (Boulder, CO: Westview Press, 1995), 159, citing Peter Conrad and Joseph W. Schneider, *Deviance and Medicalization: From Badness to Sickness* (Philadelphia: Temple University Press, 1980).

38 Stephen Katz and Barbara Marshall, "New Sex for Old: Lifestyle, Consumerism, and the Ethics of Aging Well," *Journal of Aging Studies* 17, no. 1 (2003): 4.

39 Barbara L. Marshall, "Medicalization and the Refashioning of Age-Related Limits on Sexuality," *Journal of Sex Research* 49, no. 4 (2012): 338.

40 Katz and Marshall, "New Sex for Old," 4.

41 Katz and Marshall, "New Sex for Old," 4.

42 Marshall and Katz, "Forever Functional"; Katz and Marshall, "New Sex for Old."

43 Eli Coleman, "A New Sexual Revolution in Health, Diversity and Rights," *SIECUS Report* 28, no. 2 (1999/2000): 5, quoted in Marshall, "Medicalization," 337.

44 Marshall, "Medicalization," 337.

45 Marshall, "Medicalization," 341.

46 Marshall, "Medicalization," 337.

47 Marshall and Katz, "Forever Functional," 60.

48 Wentzell, "Bad Bedfellows," 375.

49 Tiina Vares, "Reading the 'Sexy Oldie': Gender, Age(ing) and Embodiment," *Sexualities* 12, no. 4 (2009): 503–24.

50 Marshall, "Medicalization," 341.

51 Katz and Marshall, "New Sex for Old," 13.

52 For an excellent study of Freud's sense of aging as castration, see chapter 2, "Reading Freud: Aging, Castration, and Inertia," in Kathleen Woodward, *Aging and Its Discontents: Freud and Other Fictions* (Bloomington: Indiana University Press, 1991).

Conclusion

1 Linn Sandberg, "The Old, the Ugly and the Queer: Thinking Old Age in Relation to Queer Theory," *Graduate Journal of Social Science* 5, no. 2 (2008): 118. I am grateful to Sandberg, who, after we met at the Aging-Graz conference in April 2017, sent me copies of her work.

2 Sandberg's doctoral thesis on late-life male sexuality is published as *Getting Intimate: A Feminist Analysis of Old Age, Masculinity and Sexuality* (Linköping, Sweden: Linköping University, 2011).

3 Sandberg, "The Old, the Ugly and the Queer," 118.

4 Margaret Morganroth Gullette, *Agewise: Fighting the New Ageism in America* (Chicago: University of Chicago Press, 2011), 143.

5 Joan Nestle, "A Change of Life," in *A Restricted Country* (Ithaca, NY: Firebrand Books, 1987), 131–32.

6 Gullette, *Agewise*, 95. This is discussed in the present book's introduction, in the section titled "Aging and the Phallus."

BIBLIOGRAPHY

Asencio, Marysol, Thomas Blank, Lara Descartes, and Ashley Crawford. "The Prospect of Prostate Cancer: A Challenge for Gay Men's Sexualities as They Age." *Sexuality Research and Social Policy Journal* 6, no. 4 (2009): 38–51.

Barber, Stephen M., and David L. Clark. "Queer Moments: The Performative Temporalities of Eve Kosofsky Sedgwick." In *Regarding Sedgwick: Essays on Queer Culture and Critical Theory*, edited by Stephen M. Barber and David L. Clark, 1–54. Abingdon, UK: Routledge, 2002.

Belk, Russell W. "Shoes and Self." *Advances in Consumer Research* 30 (2003): 27–33.

Bersani, Leo. *The Freudian Body.* New York: Columbia University Press, 1986.

Bérubé, Michael. "Afterword." In *Disability Studies: Enabling the Humanities*, edited by Sharon Snyder, Brenda Jo Brueggemann, and Rosemarie Garland-Thomson, 337–43. New York: Modern Language Association, 2002.

Brooks, Peter. *Reading for the Plot: Design and Intention in Narrative.* Cambridge, MA: Harvard University Press, 1992.

Brown, Maria T. "LGBT Aging and Rhetorical Silence." *Sexuality Research and Social Policy: Journal of NSRC* 6, no. 4 (2009): 65–78.

Brownmiller, Susan. *Femininity.* London: Grafton Books, 1986.

Butler, Judith. *Bodies That Matter: On the Discursive Limits of "Sex."* Abingdon, UK: Routledge, 1993.

Butler, Judith. "The Lesbian Phallus and the Morphological Imaginary." *differences* 4, no. 1 (1992): 133–71.

Campbell, Jan. *Arguing with the Phallus: Feminist, Queer and Postcolonial Theory*. London: Zed Books, 2000.

Chandler, Eliza. "Sidewalk Stories: The Troubling Task of Identification." *Disability Studies Quarterly* 30, nos. 3–4 (2010). http://dsq-sds.org/article /view/1293/1329.

Clare, Eli. *Exile and Pride: Disability, Queerness and Liberation*. Classics edition. Boston: South End, 2009.

Clare, Eli. "Stolen Bodies, Reclaimed Bodies: Disability and Queerness." *Public Culture* 13, no. 3 (2001): 359–65.

Coleman, Eli. "A New Sexual Revolution in Health, Diversity and Rights." *SIECUS Report* 28, no. 2 (1999/2000): 4–8.

Conrad, Joseph. *Selected Literary Criticism and "The Shadow-Line."* Edited by Allan Ingram. London: Methuen, 1986.

Conrad, Peter, and Joseph W. Schneider. *Deviance and Medicalization: From Badness to Sickness*. Philadelphia: Temple University Press, 1980.

de Lauretis, Teresa. *The Practice of Love: Lesbian Sexuality and Perverse Desire*. Bloomington: Indiana University Press, 1994.

de Lauretis, Teresa. "Queer Theory: Lesbian and Gay Sexualities. An Introduction." *differences* 3, no. 2 (1991): iii–xviii.

Dowsett, Gary W. "'Losing My Chestnut': One Gay Man's Wrangle with Prostate Cancer." *Reproductive Health Matters* 16, no. 32 (2008): 145–50.

Early, Gerald. "Black Men and Middle Age." *Hungry Mind Review* 46, no. 1 (1993): 26.

Edelman, Lee. *No Future: Queer Theory and the Death Drive*. Durham, NC: Duke University Press, 2004.

Finkelstein, S. Naomi. "The Only Thing You Have to Do Is Live." *GLQ: A Journal of Lesbian and Gay Studies* 9, nos. 1–2 (2003): 307–19.

Franklin, Cynthia. *Academic Lives: Memoir, Cultural Theory, and the University Today*. Athens: University of Georgia Press, 2009.

Freeman, Elizabeth, ed. "Queer Temporalities." Special issue, *GLQ: A Journal of Lesbian and Gay Studies* 13, nos. 2–3 (2007).

Freeman, Elizabeth. "Time Binds, or, Erotohistoriography." *Social Text* 23, nos. 3–4 (2005): 57–68.

Freeman, Elizabeth. *Time Binds: Queer Temporalities, Queer Histories*. Durham, NC: Duke University Press, 2010.

Freud, Sigmund. "The Infantile Genital Organization: An Interpolation into the Theory of Sexuality." Translated by Joan Riviere. In *The Standard Edition of the Complete Psychological Works of Sigmund Freud*, edited by James Strachey, vol. 19, 141–48. London: Hogarth, 1961.

Freud, Sigmund. "Three Essays on the Theory of Sexuality." Translated by James Strachey. In *The Standard Edition of the Complete Psychological Works of Sigmund Freud*, edited by James Strachey, vol. 7, 125–231. London: Hogarth, 1961.

Gallop, Jane. *Anecdotal Theory*. Durham, NC: Duke University Press, 2002.

Gallop, Jane. *The Daughter's Seduction: Feminism and Psychoanalysis*. Ithaca, NY: Cornell University Press, 1982.

Gallop, Jane. *The Deaths of the Author: Reading and Writing in Time*. Durham, NC: Duke University Press, 2011.

Gallop, Jane. *Reading Lacan*. Ithaca, NY: Cornell University Press, 1985.

Gallop, Jane. *Thinking through the Body*. New York: Columbia University Press, 1987.

Gamman, Lorraine. "Self-Fashioning, Gender Display, and Sexy Girl Shoes: What's at Stake—Female Fetishism or Narcissism?" In *Footnotes: On Shoes*, edited by Shari Benstock and Suzanne Ferriss, 93–115. New Brunswick, NJ: Rutgers University Press, 2001.

Garland-Thomson, Rosemarie. *Extraordinary Bodies: Figuring Physical Disability in American Culture and Literature*. New York: Columbia University Press, 1997.

Giele, Janet Z. and Glen H. Elder Jr., eds. *Methods of Life Course Research: Qualitative and Quantitative Approaches*. Thousand Oaks, CA: Sage, 1998.

Gill, Carol. "A Psychological View of Disability Culture." *Disability Studies Quarterly* 15, no. 4 (1995): 16–19.

Gullette, Margaret Morganroth. *Aged by Culture*. Chicago: University of Chicago Press, 2004.

Gullette, Margaret Morganroth. *Agewise: Fighting the New Ageism in America*. Chicago: University of Chicago Press, 2011.

Gullette, Margaret Morganroth. *Declining to Decline: Cultural Combat and the Politics of the Midlife*. Charlottesville: University Press of Virginia, 1997.

Gullette, Margaret Morganroth. "Midlife Discourses in the Twentieth-Century United States: An Essay on the Sexuality, Ideology, and Politics of 'Middle-Ageism.'" In *Welcome to Middle Age! (And Other Cultural Fictions)*, edited by Richard A. Shweder, 3–44. Chicago: University of Chicago Press, 1998.

Gullette, Margaret Morganroth. *Safe at Last in the Middle Years: The Invention of the Midlife Progress Novel*. BackinPrint edition. New York: Authors Guild, 2000. Orig. pub. Berkeley: University of California Press, 1988.

Halberstam, Judith [Jack]. *In a Queer Time and Place: Transgender Bodies, Subcultural Lives, Sexual Cultures*. New York: New York University Press, 2005.

Halperin, David M., and Valerie Traub. "Beyond Gay Pride." In *Gay Shame*, edited by David M. Halperin and Valerie Traub, 3–40. Chicago: University of Chicago Press, 2009.

Henry, Astrid. *Not My Mother's Sister: Generational Conflict and Third-Wave Feminism*. Bloomington: Indiana University Press, 2004.

Hess, Linda M. "'My Whole Life I've Been Dressing Up Like a Man': Negotiations of Queer Aging and Queer Temporality in the TV Series *Transparent*." *European Journal of American Studies* 11, no. 3 (2017): 1–19.

Hsieh, Lili. "A Queer Sex, or, Can Feminism and Psychoanalysis Have Sex without the Phallus." *Feminist Review*, no. 102 (2012): 97–115.

Jackson, Margaret. "Sex Research and the Construction of Sexuality: A Tool of Male Supremacy?" *Women's Studies International Forum* 7, no. 1 (1984): 43–51.

Kafer, Alison. *Feminist, Queer, Crip*. Bloomington: Indiana University Press, 2013.

Katz, Stephen, and Barbara Marshall. "New Sex for Old: Lifestyle, Consumerism, and the Ethics of Aging Well." *Journal of Aging Studies* 17, no. 1 (2003): 3–16.

King, Amy M. "Dilatory Description and the Pleasures of Accumulation." In *Narrative Middles*, edited by Caroline Levine and Mario Ortiz-Robles, 161–94. Columbus: Ohio State University Press, 2013.

Lacan, Jacques. "The Signification of the Phallus." In *Écrits: A Selection*, translated by Alan Sheridan, 281–91. New York: Norton, 1977.

Lacan, Jacques. "Tuche and Automaton." In *The Four Fundamental Concepts of Psycho-Analysis*, translated by Alan Sheridan, 53–66. New York: Norton, 1978.

Lawrence, D. H. *Lady Chatterley's Lover*. New York: Bantam Classic, 2007.

Lehrer, Riva. "Golem Girl Gets Lucky." In *Sex and Disability*, edited by Robert McRuer and Anna Mollow, 231–55. Durham, NC: Duke University Press, 2012.

Marshall, Barbara L. "Medicalization and the Refashioning of Age-Related Limits on Sexuality." *Journal of Sex Research* 49, no. 4 (2012): 337–43.

Marshall, Barbara L., and Stephen Katz. "Forever Functional: Sexual Fitness and the Ageing Male Body." *Body and Society* 8, no. 4 (2002): 43–70.

McPhillips, Kathryn, Virginia Braun, and Nicola Gavey. "Defining (Hetero) Sex: How Imperative Is the 'Coital Imperative'?" *Women's Studies International Forum* 24, no. 2 (2001): 229–40.

McRuer, Robert. *Crip Theory: Cultural Signs of Queerness and Disability*. New York: New York University Press, 2006.

McRuer, Robert, and Anna Mollow, eds. *Sex and Disability*. Durham, NC: Duke University Press, 2012.

McRuer, Robert, and Abby L. Wilkerson, eds. "Queer Theory Meets Disability Studies." Special issue, *GLQ: A Journal of Lesbian and Gay Studies* 9, nos. 1–2 (2003).

Medovoi, Leerom. "Age Trouble: A Timely Subject in American Literary and Cultural Studies." *American Literary History* 22, no. 3 (2010): 657–72.

Mellard, James Milton. "Gifts Reserved for Age: A Lacanian Study of Comedy in Philip Roth's *Exit Ghost*." *Acta Scientarum, Language and Culture* 32, no. 1 (2010): 7–20.

Morrison, Paul. "End Pleasure." *GLQ: A Journal of Lesbian and Gay Studies* 1, no. 1 (1993): 53–78.

Neelakantan, Gurumurthy. "Fiction as Faith: Philip Roth's Testament in *Exit Ghost*." *Philip Roth Studies* 10, no. 2 (2014): 31–45.

Nestle, Joan. "A Change of Life." In *A Restricted Country*, 131–33. Ithaca, NY: Firebrand Books, 1987.

Platt, Mary Frances. "Reclaiming Femme . . . Again." In *The Persistent Desire: A Femme-Butch Reader*, edited by Joan Nestle, 388–89. New York: Alyson, 1992.

Port, Cynthia. "No Future? Aging, Temporality, History, and Reverse Chronologies." *Occasion: Interdisciplinary Studies in the Humanities* 4 (2012): 1–19.

Rossi, William A. *The Sex Life of the Foot and the Shoe*. New York: Saturday Review Press / E. P. Dutton, 1976.

Roth, Philip. *Exit Ghost*. New York: Vintage, 2007.

Royal, Derek Parker, ed. "Zuckerman Unsound? A Roundtable Discussion on Philip Roth's *Exit Ghost*." *Philip Roth Studies* 5, no. 1 (2009): 7–34.

Sandberg, Linn. *Getting Intimate: A Feminist Analysis of Old Age, Masculinity and Sexuality*. Linköping, Sweden: Linköping University, 2011.

Sandberg, Linn. "The Old, the Ugly and the Queer: Thinking Old Age in Relation to Queer Theory." *Graduate Journal of Social Science* 5, no. 2 (2008): 117–39.

Shakespeare, Tom. "Disabled Sexuality: Toward Rights and Recognition." *Sexuality and Disability* 18, no. 3 (2000): 159–66.

Steele, Valerie. *Shoes: A Lexicon of Style*. London: Scriptum Editions, 1998.

Tiefer, Leonore. *Sex Is Not a Natural Act and Other Essays*. Boulder, CO: Westview Press, 1995.

Ullerstam, Lars. *The Erotic Minorities*. New York: Grove Press, 1966.

Updike, John. *Couples*. New York: Knopf, 1968.

Ussher, Jane M., Janette Perz, Emilee Gilbert, W. K. Tim Wong, and Kim Hobbs. "Renegotiating Sex and Intimacy after Cancer: Resisting the Coital Imperative." *Cancer Nursing* 36, no. 6 (2013): 454–62.

Vares, Tiina. "Reading the 'Sexy Oldie': Gender, Age(ing) and Embodiment." *Sexualities* 12, no. 4 (2009): 503–24.

Wachsler, Sharon. "Still Femme." In *Restricted Access: Lesbians on Disability*, edited by Victoria Brownworth and Susan Raffo, 109–14. Seattle: Seal Press, 1999.

Waxman, Barbara Faye, and Carol J. Gill. "Sexuality and Disability: Mis-state of the Arts." *Journal of Sex Research* 33, no. 3 (1996): 267–70.

Weisbord, Merrily. *Our Future Selves: Love, Life, Sex, and Aging.* Berkeley, CA: North Atlantic Books, 1991.

Wentzell, Emily. "Bad Bedfellows: Disability Sex Rights and Viagra." *Bulletin of Science, Technology and Society* 26, no. 5 (2006): 370–77.

Wilkerson, Abby. "Slipping." In *Gay Shame*, edited by David M. Halperin and Valerie Traub, 188–91. Chicago: University of Chicago Press, 2009.

Williams, Simon J. "Bodily Dys-Order: Desire, Excess and the Transgression of Corporeal Boundaries." *Body and Society* 4, no. 2 (1998): 59–82.

Wobovnik, Claudia. "These Shoes Aren't Made for Walking: Rethinking High-Heeled Shoes as Cultural Artifacts." *Visual Culture and Gender* 8 (2013): 82–92.

Woodward, Kathleen. *Aging and Its Discontents: Freud and Other Fictions.* Bloomington: Indiana University Press, 1991.

INDEX

Age, Culture, Humanities journal, 9
Aged by Culture (Gullette), 11–12
Agewise (Gullette), 7, 18–19
aging: anecdotal theory and, 29–30; coital imperative and, 86–91, 94–95; decline theory and, 61–64; disability studies and, 38–40; longitudinal aspect of sexuality and, 95–102, 108–11; phallus and, 13–20; post-prostate temporality and, 78–81; queer temporality and, 5–13, 101–2, 107–8, 115n29; sexuality and, 6–13, 96–102
Aging and Its Discontents (Woodward), 15–17
Allan, Ted, 93–94
androcentrism, psychoanalytic phallus and, 14–20
anecdotal theory: crip theory and, 25–30; gender and disability and, 56–58
Anecdotal Theory (Gallop), 26–30

artful handicap, Brownmiller's concept of, 52

"Bad Bedfellows: Disability Sex Rights and Viagra" (Wentzell), 94–95, 99
Barber, Steven M., 9
Bersani, Leo, 82
Bérubé, Michael, 5
Brooks, Peter, 65
Brown, Maria T., 7–10
Brownmiller, Susan, 51–52
butch-femme perspective, gender and disability and, 54–58, 121n46
Butler, Judith, 20–25, 122n56

Campbell, Jan, 20–23, 118n73
Cancer Nursing journal, 4, 84
castration narrative: adult-onset disability and, 58–64, 104–7; decline ideology and, 61–64; disability narrative of, 37–40; femme identity and, 55–58;

castration narrative (*continued*)
longitudinal aspect of sexuality and, 95–102, 108–11; perma-
nence in, 107–11; psychoanalytic
phallus and, 15–20; queer phallus
and concept of, 20–25; sexuality
and disability and, 37–38; shoes
and sexuality and, 50–52; temporality and, 58–66, 75–81
catastrophic loss, aging and,
38–40
catwalk metaphor, disability and
sexuality and, 42–46
Chandler, Eliza, 40–46
"Change of Life, A" (Nestle), 109–11
children, queer temporality and,
10–11
Cialis, 70–73, 98–99
"City Sidewalks" narrative, 31–36,
45–46
Clare, Eli, 1–2, 29, 52–53
Clark, David L., 9
coital imperative: pre-cum and,
81–91; resistance to, 92–95
Coleman, Eli, 98
Conrad, Joseph, 78–81, 97–98,
122n7
Couples (Updike), 17–18
Cowper's fluid: coital imperative
and, 83–91; ejaculation and, 69,
71
crip theory: aging and, 38–40; anecdotal theory and, 28–30, 118n86;
coital imperative and, 94–95; evo-
lution of, 1–4; gender and disability and, 52–58; queer temporality
and aging and, 5–13; sexuality
and disability in, 36–38
*Crip Theory: Cultural Signs of Queer-
ness and Disability* (McRuer), 1

decline theory (Gullette), 11–12;
aging and disability and, 38–40;

castration temporality and,
61–64; crip theory and, 12–13
Declining to Decline (Gullette), 11–12,
17–18, 29–30, 38–40
"Defining (Hetero)Sex: How Imperative Is the 'Coital Imperative'?"
(McPhillips et al.), 87–91
de Lauretis, Teresa, 20–21, 25
desexualization, psychoanalytic castration and, 18–20
*Diagnostic and Statistical Manual of
Mental Disorders* (*DSM*), 95
disability sex rights movement, 2–4;
coital imperative and, 84–91,
94–95
disability studies: aging and, 38–40;
anecdotal theory and, 28–30,
118n86; gender and, 52–58; high
heels and, 51–52; identity in,
40–46, 54–58; personal narrative in, 31–36; queer temporality
and aging and, 5–13; queer theory
and, 1–4; "sidewalk stories" and,
40–46
Disability Studies Quarterly, 40
Doonan, Simon, 47–48
Dowsett, Gary, 82, 92

Early, Gerald, 61–62, 66
Edelman, Lee, 10
ejaculation: coital imperative and,
81–82; prostate cancer and, 67–74
"End Pleasure" (Morrison), 81–83,
122n12
erectile function: coital imperative
and, 82–95; prostate cancer and,
67–74
Exile and Pride (Clare), 29, 52–53
Exit Ghost (Roth), 75–81, 90–102,
106–7

feminist studies: anecdotal theory
and, 26–30; coital imperative in,

87–88; resistance to coital imperative in, 92–95; shoes and, 46–52
fetish, queer phallus and, 20–25
Finkelstein, S. Naomi, 56–59
Ford, Tom, 47–48
"forever functional" ideology, 98–102, 107–11
Franklin, Cynthia, 26–30, 118n81
Freeman, Elizabeth, 8–9
Freudian theory: anecdotal theory and, 27–30; end-pleasure in, 81–82, 88; infantile sexuality in, 62–63; phallus in, 14–20, 103, 116n42; sexual development in, 86–91; temporality of sexuality in, 101–2
futurism, aging and queer temporality and, 10–11

Gamman, Lorraine, 46–52
Garland-Thomson, Rosemarie, 2
Gay Shame (Halperin and Traub), 28–29, 41–42
gender: disability and, 52–58, 64–66; late-onset disability and, 15–20
gerontology, queer temporality and, 7–8
Gilbert, Emilee, 4
Gill, Carol, 3
GLQ journal, 55–56, 81
Gullette, Margaret Morganroth: anecdotal theory and, 29–30; crip theory and influence of, 5, 7–10; decline theory of, 11–13, 38–40, 61–62, 66, 105, 116n36, 117n50; longitudinal concept of sexuality and, 108–9; on psychoanalytic castration, 17–19

Halberstam, Judith (Jack), 8–9
Hess, Linda M., 115n29
high-heeled shoes, feminism and, 46–52

Hobbs, Kim, 4
homosexuality, depathologization of, 94–95
Hsieh, Lili, 22–25

identity, longitudinal identities, 95–102, 107–11
impotence: medicalization of, 96–102; prostate cancer and, 67–74; resistance to coital imperative and, 92–95
inexorability, sexuality and disability and, 39–40
infantile sexuality, Freudian concept of, 62–63
institutionalized life course, queer temporality and, 7–8, 10–12

Katz, Stephen, 6, 96–98, 100–102, 106–7
King, Amy M., 122n12

Lacanian theory, phallus in, 14–20, 23–24, 103
Lady Chatterley's Lover (Lawrence), 37–38, 58–60, 62–66, 105
late-onset disability: aging and, 5–13, 103–7; castration temporality and, 58–66; sexuality and, 15–20
Lawrence, D. H., 37–38, 58–59, 62–64
Lehrer, Riva, 2–3, 42–44, 53–54; on aging and disability, 6
lesbianism: disability and femme identity and, 54–58; normative sexuality and, 59–64
"lesbian phallus," Butler's concept of, 20–25, 118n68, 122n56
"Lesbian Phallus and the Morphological Imaginary, The" (Butler), 21–22
longitudinal sexuality, 95–102, 107–11

Marshall, Barbara, 6, 96–102, 106–7
McRuer, Robert, 1
Medovoi, Leerom, 116n36
Mellard, James Milton, 76–77
menopause, Freudian concept of castration and, 18–19, 117n54
Modern Language Association (mla), 5–6
Morrison, Paul, 81–83, 88

Nestle, Joan, 109–11, 121n46
No Future (Edelman), 10–11
noncoital sex: coital imperative and, 86–91; enjoyment of, 92–95
normative mobility, gender and disability and, 52–58
normativity: disability studies and, 2, 64–66; phallic sexuality and, 59–64, 104–7; queer temporality and, 8
Nyong'o, Tavia, 23

"Old, the Ugly, and the Queer, The" (Sandberg), 7
orgasm: coital imperative and, 83–91; disability and, 56–59; ejaculation and, 69, 71

pelvic wellness, sexuality and, 72–74
penis: high heels as replacement for, 48–49; queer phallus and, 20–25
Persistent Desire, The (Nestle), 121n46
personal narrative: anecdotal theory and, 25–30; coital imperative and, 82–91; disability in, 31–36; end-pleasure in, 81–83, 122n12
Perz, Janette, 4
phallic surprise, sexuality and disability and, 37–38, 64–66
phallus: aging and, 13–20; disability and, 36–38; Freudian sexual

development and, 86–91; high heels and, 48–52; queer phallus, 20–25; temporality of, 62–66, 74–81, 103–7; in wheelchair, 58–64
Platt, Mary Frances, 54, 57–58
Port, Cynthia, 9–11, 115n29
postmenopausal sexuality, 8
poststructuralism, anecdotal theory and, 26–30
pre-cum: coital imperative and, 81–91, 106–7; prostate cancer and, 74–81
private body, public world and, 40–46
prostate cancer, sexuality and, 67–74
psychoanalysis: anecdotal theory and, 27–30; femme identity in, 55–56; phallus in, 13–20, 103–7; queer phallus and, 21–25; shoes and sexuality and, 49–52
public world, private body and, 40–46

"Queering the Phallus" (Campbell), 20–23
queer temporality: aging and, 101–2, 107–8; defined, 7–10, 115n29; gender and disability and, 57–58; phallic surprise and, 64–66, 103–4
queer theory: aging and temporality in, 5–13; anecdotal theory and, 28–30; disability studies and, 1–4; medicalization of sexuality and, 96; queer phallus in, 20–25; resistance to coital imperative in, 92–95

"Reclaiming Femme . . . Again" (Platt), 57–58
"Renegotiating Sex and Intimacy

after Cancer" (Ussher et al.), 4, 84–87, 92–95
reproductivity: futurism and, 10; phallic sexuality and, 59–64
Rossi, William A., 49–51, 120n33
Roth, Philip, 75–81, 90–91, 93–102, 106–7

Safe at Last in the Middle Years (Gullette), 17–18
Sandberg, Linn, 7, 107–8
Sedgwick, Eve, 9
Sex and Disability (Lehrer), 2
Sex Life of the Foot and the Shoe, The (Rossi), 49–50
sexual identity, crip theory and, 2–4
sexuality: aging and, 6–13, 96–102, 104–7; anecdotal theory and, 27–30; disability studies and, 2–4, 42–46, 56–58, 64–66; high heels and, 47–52; longitudinal aspect of, 95–102, 108–11; phallus and, 14–20; prostate cancer and, 67–74
Sexuality and Disability journal, 3–4
Shadow-Line, The (Conrad), 78–81, 97–98
Shakespeare, Tom, 3–4
shoes: disability studies and, 31–36, 45–46, 120n33; feminism and, 46–52
Shoes: A Lexicon of Style (Steele), 46
"sidewalk stories," 40–46
"Silver Bells" (song), 45–46
"Slipping" (Wilkerson), 28–29

temporality: castration and, 58–66; decline theory and, 61–64; denial of, 100–101; phallus and, 62–66, 74–81; sexuality and, 95–102, 107–11
Three Essays on the Theory of Sexuality (Freud), 101–2
Tiefer, Leonore, 96

Updike, John, 17–18
Ussher, Jane M., 4

Vares, Tiina, 100
Viagra, sexuality and aging and, 94–95, 98–102

Wachsler, Sharon, 54–58
walking: anecdotal theory and, 36–40; disability and, 40–46
Waxman, Barbara, 3
Wentzell, Emily, 3, 13, 94–95, 99–101
wheelchair: castration and, 36–38; femme identity and, 54; phallus in, 58–64, 105–7
Wilkerson, Abby, 28–29
Wobovnik, Claudia, 47–48, 50–51
women, castration theory and, 15–20
Women's Studies International Forum, 85
Wong, W. K. Tim, 4
Woodward, Kathleen, 15–17, 19–20, 117n50